IT'S EVEN WORSE
THAN IT LOOKS

IT'S EVEN WORSE THAN IT LOOKS

HOW THE AMERICAN CONSTITUTIONAL SYSTEM COLLIDED WITH THE NEW POLITICS OF EXTREMISM

THOMAS E. MANN AND NORMAN J. ORNSTEIN

BASIC BOOKS
A MEMBER OF THE PERSEUS BOOKS GROUP
NEW YORK

Published by Basic Books,
A Member of the Perseus Books Group

Books published by Basic Books are available at special discounts for
bulk purchases in the United States by corporations, institutions, and
other organizations. For more information, please contact the Special
Markets Department at the Perseus Books Group, 2300 Chestnut Street,
Suite 200, Philadelphia, PA 19103, or call (800) 810-4145, ext. 5000,
or e-mail special.markets@perseusbooks.com.

Design and production by Eclipse Publishing Services

A CIP catalog record for this book is available
from the Library of Congress.

Hardcover ISBN: 978-0-465-03133-7
E-book ISBN: 978-0-465-03136-8

10 9 8 7 6 5 4 3 2

To our terrific families who keep both of us grounded–
Sheilah, Stephanie, and Ted, Suzanne and Leonardo;
and Judy, Matthew, Danny, and Harvey

And in memory of our dear friend and
prescient scholar, Austin Ranney

Contents

Introduction

On January 26, 2010, the Senate voted on a resolution to create an eighteen-member deficit-reduction task force with teeth, a fast-track procedure to bring a sweeping plan to solve the U.S.'s debt problem straight to the floor for an up-or-down vote. The resolution was coauthored by Democrat Kent Conrad of North Dakota and Republican Judd Gregg of New Hampshire, and had substantial bipartisan support, including from Republican leaders like John McCain and Mitch McConnell. The latter did not cosponsor the resolution but had said eight months earlier on the Senate floor:

> We must address the issue of entitlement spending now before it is too late. As I have said many times before, the best way to address the crisis is the Conrad-Gregg proposal, which would provide an expedited pathway for fixing these profound long-term challenges. This plan would force us to get debt and spending under control. It deserves support from both sides of the aisle. The administration

has expressed a desire to take up entitlement reform, and given the debt that its budget would run up, the need for reform has never been greater. So I urge the administration, once again, to support the Conrad-Gregg proposal. This proposal is our best hope for addressing the out-of-control spending and debt levels that are threatening our nation's fiscal future.[1]

But on January 26, the Senate blocked the resolution. Fifty-three senators supported it, but it could not garner the sixty votes needed to overcome a Republican filibuster. Among those who voted to sustain the filibuster and kill the resolution were Mitch McConnell and John McCain. McCain was joined in opposition by six other original cosponsors, all Republicans. Never before have cosponsors of a major bill conspired to kill their own idea, in an almost Alice-in-Wonderland fashion. Why did they do so? Because President Barack Obama was for it, and its passage might gain him political credit.

Fred Hiatt, the opinion editor of the *Washington Post*, wrote of McConnell's change of position, "No single vote by any single senator could possibly illustrate everything that is wrong with Washington today. No single vote could embody the full cynicism and cowardice of our political elite at its worst, or explain by itself why problems do not get solved. But here's one that comes close."[2]

• • •

Six years ago, we wrote *The Broken Branch*, which sharply criticized the Congress for failing to live up to its responsibilities as the first branch of government. Based on four decades of watching Congress, ours was a sympathetic perspective, one that reflected our appreciation of the inherent messiness of the legislative process within the constitutional system. Reconciling diverse interests and beliefs in America's extended republic necessarily involves adversarial debates and difficult negotiations.

But there was no denying the impact of broad changes in America's wider political environment—most importantly the ideological polarization of the political parties—on how Congress went about its work. We documented the demise of regular order, as Congress bent rules to marginalize committees and deny the minority party in the House opportunities to offer amendments on the floor; the decline of genuine deliberation in the lawmaking process on such important matters as budgets and decisions to go to war; the manifestations of extreme partisanship; the culture of corruption; the loss of institutional patriotism among members; and the weakening of the checks-and-balances system.

While we observed some improvement after the Democrats regained control of Congress in the 2006 midterm elections, the most problematic features of the system remained. We thought them unlikely to abate absent a major national crisis that inspired the American public to demand that the warring parties work together. America got the crisis—the most serious economic downturn since the Great Depression—and a pretty clear signal from the voters, who elected Barack Obama by a comfortable margin and gave the Democrats substantial gains in the House and Senate. What the country didn't get was any semblance of a well-functioning democracy. President Obama's postpartisan pitch fell flat, and the Tea Party movement pulled the GOP further to its ideological pole. Republicans greeted the new president with a unified strategy of opposing, obstructing, discrediting, and nullifying every one of his important initiatives. Obama reaped an impressive legislative harvest in his first two years but without any Republican engagement or support and with no apparent appreciation from the public. The anemic economic recovery and the pain of joblessness and underwater home mortgages led not to any signal that the representatives ought to pull together, but rather to yet another call by voters to "throw the bums out." The Democrats' devastating setback in the 2010 midterm elections, in which they lost six Senate seats and sixty-three in the House, produced a Republican majority in the House dominated by right-wing insurgents determined to radically reduce the size and role of government. What followed was an appalling spectacle of hostage taking—most importantly, the debt ceiling crisis—that threatened a government shutdown and public default, led to a downgrading of the country's credit, and blocked constructive action to nurture an economic recovery or deal with looming problems of deficits and debt.

In October 2011, Congress garnered its lowest approval rating (9 percent) in polling history. Public trust in the government's capacity to solve the serious problems facing the country also hit record lows. Almost all Americans felt their country was on the wrong track and were pessimistic about the future. The public viewed both parties negatively, and President Obama's job approval rating was mired in the forties. The widespread consensus was that politics and governance were utterly dysfunctional. In spite of the perilous state of the global economy—and with it the threat of another financial crisis and recession—no one expected the president and Congress to accomplish anything of consequence before the 2012 election.[3]

Paradoxically, the public's undifferentiated disgust with Congress, Washington, and "the government" in general is part of the problem, not the basis of a solution. In never-ending efforts to defeat incumbent officeholders in hard times, the public is perpetuating the source of its discontent, electing a new group of people who are even less inclined to or capable of crafting compromise or solutions to pressing problems. We have been struck by the failure of the media, including editors, reporters, and many "expert" commentators, to capture the real drivers of these disturbing developments, and the futility of efforts by many nonpartisan and bipartisan groups to counter, much less overcome, them. We write this book to try to clarify the source of dysfunctional politics and what it will take to change it. The stakes involved in choosing who will lead us in the White House, the Congress, and the Supreme Court in the years ahead are unusually high, given both the gravity of the problems and the sharper polarization of the parties.

In the pages that follow, we identify two overriding sources of dysfunction. The first is the serious mismatch between the political parties, which have become as vehemently adversarial as parliamentary parties, and a governing system that, unlike a parliamentary democracy, makes it extremely difficult for majorities to act. Parliamentary-style parties in a separation-of-powers government are a formula for willful obstruction and policy irresolution. Sixty years ago, Austin Ranney, an eminent political scientist, wrote a prophetic dissent to a famous report by an American Political Science Association committee entitled "Toward a More Responsible Two-Party System."[4] The report, by prominent political scientists frustrated with the role of conservative Southern Democrats in blocking civil rights and other social policy, issued a clarion call for more ideologically coherent, internally unified, and adversarial parties in the fashion of a Westminster-style parliamentary democracy like Britain or Canada. Ranney powerfully argued that such parties would be a disaster within the American constitutional system, given our separation of powers, separately elected institutions, and constraints on majority rule that favor cross-party coalitions and compromise. Time has proven Ranney dead right—we now have the kinds of parties the report desired, and it is disastrous.

The second is the fact that, however awkward it may be for the traditional press and nonpartisan analysts to acknowledge, one of the two major parties, the Republican Party, has become an insurgent outlier—ideologically extreme; contemptuous of the inherited social and economic policy regime; scornful of compromise; unpersuaded by conventional understanding of facts, evidence, and science; and dismissive of the legitimacy of its political opposition. When one party moves this far from the center of American politics, it is extremely difficult to enact policies responsive to the country's most pressing challenges.

Recognizing these two realities and understanding how America got here is key to taking the right steps to overcome dysfunctional politics.

PART I

The Problem

The New Politics of Hostage Taking

The story we recount in our introduction, when seven original cosponsors of a tough Senate resolution to create a deficit-reduction panel voted against the plan in January 2010, solely because President Barack Obama, a Democrat, had endorsed it, underscores how out of whack American politics and policy making have become. But the debt limit crisis eighteen months later—in which Republican party leaders cynically decided to hold hostage America's full faith and credit in a reckless game of chicken with the president—moved the dysfunction gauge sharply into the danger zone.

The debt limit crisis of 2011 inspired as much coverage as any political story of the year, but we believe we need to revisit it, from its genesis on, to understand its future implications. The crisis underscored for many Americans the utter dysfunction in our politics and the disdain of our elected officials for finding solutions to big problems. To be sure, prolonged and contentious negotiations over important policies are not new, and the endgames usually go right up to the deadlines, and occasionally beyond. But these negotiations were so prolonged and contentious, and involved so many threats by top leaders that they would, according to Jason Chaffetz of Utah, "have taken it [the debt limit and America's credit] down" unless the Republicans' inflexible demands were met. The final deal to raise the ceiling left a clear impression that the next time might well be worse.

Watching the debt limit debacle unfold led us to our title for this book: *It's Even Worse Than It Looks*. As bad as the atmospherics were, the new and enhanced politics of hostage taking, of putting political expedience above the national interest and tribal hubris above cooperative problem solving, suggested something more dangerous, especially at a time of profound economic peril.

The short-term consequences of the standoff were serious, as Standard & Poor's downgraded the U.S. credit rating for the first time in history, noting that "[t]he political brinkmanship of recent months highlights what we see as America's governance and policy making becoming less stable, less effective, and less predictable than what we previously believed."[1] Federal Reserve Chairman Ben Bernanke weighed in as well, with unusually pointed criticism of Congress: "The negotiations that took place over the summer disrupted financial markets and probably the economy as well."[2] Voters were, if anything, even angrier; a *New York Times* survey completed after the votes showed the highest disapproval levels for Congress since it began recording them, at 82 percent, with Republicans suffering voters' unhappiness more than Democrats.[3]

• • •

The debt limit is a vestigial organ created in 1917 to facilitate Congress's ability to raise money on the eve of America's entry into World War I. Until then, Congress had to appropriate money through short-term debt instruments, like Treasury bills. So a device to enable Congress to issue longer-term debt instruments, even for specific appropriations, both lowered interest costs and made the borrowing easier for the Treasury Department. The process was altered to pull all spending requirements together and create a single, overall debt limit in 1939.

There are other ways to deal with the problem of raising money besides nineteenth-century methods, including the passage of a budget (something which Congress did not do until after enactment of the 1973 Budget and Impoundment Control Act). Since the debt limit simply accommodates debt that has already been incurred, raising it should, in theory, be perfunctory. But politicians have found it a useful shibboleth for showing their fealty to fiscal discipline, even as they vote to ratify the debts their previous actions have obligated the country to pay. The symbol of railing against debt has proven politically beneficial, even if not substantively meaningful.

Congressional efforts to raise the debt limit are not rare events. Between 1960 and August 2011, Congress had done so seventy-eight times, forty-nine times with Republican presidents and twenty-nine with Democrats in the White House.[4] Many efforts to raise the debt limit were contentious, and not a few pushed the issue to the brink, going right up to the date at which the Treasury Department declared that default would occur absent congressional action. Indeed, in 2002, Congress pushed well past the point at which the Treasury said the formal debt limit would be breached and after it had exhausted most of the informal measures, such as borrowing temporarily from federal retirement accounts. With the prospects of default looming, the House passed an increase in the debt limit by a single vote.

Most votes on the debt limit, including the one in 2002, were partisan. Lawmakers' votes could be predicted best by looking at whether they shared party identification with the incumbent president. Most votes involved overheated rhetoric, either in the service of fiscal discipline or in the dire consequences of denigrating the full faith and credit of the United States. Notably, many on both sides of the aisle had a history of voting for and/or arguing both sides of the issue at different times, including leaders like Nancy Pelosi, John Boehner, and, yes, then Senator Barack Obama (who voted against raising the debt limit when George W. Bush was president). Many of the votes involved razor-thin margins. On several occasions, most recently in 1977, the eleventh-hour votes did not leave enough time to finish the formalities of enacting bills into law, resulting in a technical default (i.e., no legal authority for the government to pay its bills) for a matter of hours. But, as evidence of the underlying danger of the issue, this modest technical default—no bills went unpaid—actually resulted in a rise in interest rates because it led to questions about America's reliability in its promises to lenders.

Pyrotechnics and symbols aside, on every occasion on which the government needed to raise the debt ceiling, the key actors in Washington, including presidents and congressional leaders, knew that almost nobody—until now—had any intention of precipitating a default. Leaders of the president's party told us privately on the eve of more than one ostensibly nail-biting vote, including in 2002, that they knew in advance that their counterpart's members, along with some of their own antsy colleagues, were willing to switch if it looked as if the debt limit vote might actually fail with the deadline looming. Until 2011, both parties tacitly accepted the hypocritical political posturing that always accompanies the debt limit discussion, even as it brought heartburn to the president and his congressional leaders, who would have preferred not to rely on the private promises of reluctant lawmakers afraid of attack ads hitting them for fiscal profligacy. And until 2011, when Republicans insisted that the president and Democrats cave in to their demands on sweeping spending cuts (and no tax increases), no debt limit increase had any preconditions attached.

Frustrated by the drama accompanying debt limit votes, both Republican and Democratic leaders frequently invoked the so-called Gephardt Rule (named after its author, former Majority Leader Richard Gephardt of Missouri), which, starting in 1980, automatically increased the debt limit with passage of a budget resolution that itself set spending and taxing levels.

When the Republicans took the House in 1995, they waived the Gephardt Rule, setting up a confrontation with President Bill Clinton, but they blinked when it came to breaching the debt limit and instead sought to use the threat to shut down the government to reduce spending. (The result was two partial government shutdowns and a huge backlash against the Republicans.) In 2011, after retaking the House, Republicans did more than waive the Gephardt Rule. They repealed it, setting up a new and more serious confrontation.

We know now that the result of the 2011 debt limit fandango was by no means preordained. The Republican Party leaders did not have guaranteed votes to pull out just in time, nor were they playing the usual political games to gain more traction on the argument for greater fealty to fiscal discipline. For the first time, major political figures, including top congressional leaders and serious presidential candidates, openly called for default or demanded dramatic and unilateral policy changes in return for preserving the full faith and credit of the United States. For some members, including but not limited to Tea Party freshmen, the real threat of Armageddon was a way of spurning "politics as usual," of showing they would operate outside the old-boy network of standard Washington practices. For Republican leaders, the hope was that the genuine threat of breaching the debt limit would force the president to cave, giving them both a substantive and, more importantly, a political victory over a weak president forced to bend to their will. They were joined by major outside opinion leaders like hedge fund manager Stan Druckenmiller, a staunch conservative, who told the *Wall Street Journal* that he had no fear of a default—that he was more uneasy about a deal between the parties that would compromise his ideology.[5]

The Young Guns

A key to the new dynamic was in the new generation of Republican leaders in the House—a group calling themselves the "Young Guns," the name alone demonstrating their swagger and commitment to new confrontational politics and in-your-face tactics designed to distinguish them from both their compromising predecessors and their accommodating senior colleagues.[6] Led by incoming Majority Leader Eric Cantor of Virginia, the Republican Young Guns were an interesting and unusual phenomenon. The parties have often had young turks rebelling against their leaders and pushing for bolder, simpler, and more confrontational solutions or actions. These young turks were not outsiders, however, but core members of their own party establishment and key figures high up in the party leadership. They had lofty ideological goals combined with fierce personal ambition. That combination made it much harder for Speaker of the

House John Boehner of Ohio to operate as a negotiator with the president or Democrats in the House or to forge a common leadership position to contain the right-wing forces from the Tea Party and the conservative caucus called the Republican Study Committee within his own ranks. For a year or more, the Young Guns had plotted a confrontation over the debt limit that would not be an idle threat but a real bludgeon to force radical policy change in one fell swoop.

Thus, the hostage crisis began. Of course, an effective hostage-taking operation requires hostage takers to convince their adversaries that they will follow through if their demands are not met. That credible threat was a core part of what made 2011 different from previous confrontations over the debt limit.

At the root of the threat was Eric Cantor's rise through House Republican leadership ranks and his ambitious plan, hatched soon after Barack Obama's 2008 victory with his two Young Gun colleagues, Kevin McCarthy of California and Paul Ryan of Wisconsin. They planned to recruit a new generation of highly ideological and uncompromising conservative candidates for the 2010 elections, provide them with money and technical support, and keep the focus on fiscal issues. The fiscal issues served two goals: they were meant to reinforce voters' unhappiness with Washington and the economy, and to accomplish a greater end, decreasing—by any means necessary—the size of government to pre–1960s Great Society levels.

At the Young Guns' urging, many of those candidates began early in the 2010 campaign to talk about the debt ceiling as a core symbol of all that was wrong with Washington. They frequently mischaracterized a vote to lift the debt ceiling as a vote to add more debt. The Young Guns also appealed to the Tea Party movement that had emerged in 2009, fanning the seething populist anger that many activist conservatives felt. Ryan, Cantor, and McCarthy wrote a book in the fall of 2010—called, naturally, *Young Guns: A New Generation of Conservative Leaders*—that was a manifesto of their tough conservative views, including large tax cuts to starve the beast of big government. The book also conspicuously failed to mention the top House Republican leader, John Boehner, a sign of tensions to come.

Of course, the Young Guns' strategy fit nicely with the sweeping Republican victory in the 2010 midterm elections. Cantor became House Majority Leader, McCarthy emerged as the choice for Majority Whip, and Ryan became chairman-elect of the House Budget Committee. Non–Young Gun Boehner became Speaker-elect of the House.

With eighty-seven freshmen, most elected with Tea Party backing, Boehner knew that his job as Speaker, which made him responsible for governing, would be especially challenging. And he knew even before he was sworn in that the debt limit would be a critical test. Two weeks after the election, Boehner was quoted as saying of his freshmen and the debt limit, "I've made it pretty clear to them that as we get into next year, it's pretty clear that Congress is going to have to deal with [it]." He added, "We're going to have to deal with it as adults. Whether we like it or not, the federal government has obligations, and we have obligations on our part."[7]

Of course, neither the freshmen nor the Young Guns received this message well, and Cantor was especially resistant to the idea of swallowing hard and accepting the responsibility that comes with being in the majority. Soon after the election, Utah's second-term firebrand Jason Chaffetz talked to Cantor about how the new majority would use its power. Based on an interview with Chaffetz, a *Washington Post* story recounts, "Cantor didn't hesitate. He said, 'One of the biggest things that's going to happen is that we have to deal with the debt ceiling.' Said Chaffetz, 'He, in particular, knew a long time ago that was going to be a big deal.'" In other words, Cantor was prepared to make a stand on the debt limit and dare President Obama and the Democrats either to accept his demands or to live with the economic consequences of a debt limit breach. That was not the approach Speaker Boehner wanted to pursue, but it appealed to a sizable group of restive House Republicans eager for a revolution.

In January 2011, the newly installed House majority gathered in Baltimore for a retreat. Here, Cantor made his intentions clear, giving the message—counter to what the Speaker-elect had warned after the election—directly to his full party caucus. He implored them to use the coming debt limit vote as their golden opportunity to force the White House to bend to their will and dramatically cut spending: "I'm asking you to look at a potential increase in the debt limit as a leverage moment when the White House and President Obama will have to deal with us." He added, "Either we stick together and demonstrate that we're a team that will fight for and stand by our principles, or we will lose that leverage."[8]

Cantor did not confine his pitch to the debt limit. He outlined a three-prong strategy for confrontation with the president. The first prong would be the continuing resolution needed to keep much of the government funded through the remainder of fiscal year 2011, which had started the previous October 1. The second prong would be the debt limit, and the third, the spending bills for the next fiscal year, starting October 1, 2011.

When Congress is unable to complete its spending bills on time, it passes a resolution to continue spending, usually at the previous year's levels, as a stopgap measure. But no continuing resolution means no spending—and a government shutdown. Due to both the heavy substantive agenda in the second session of the 111th Congress (including health-care reform and the Dodd-Frank financial regulation) and to Republicans' delay and obstruction, Congress had enacted not one of the twelve appropriations bills funding agencies and programs from health research to education to transportation to homeland security for the new fiscal year. And the continuing resolutions enacted for fiscal year 2011 had, at Republican insistence, been of much shorter duration than is typical. Six separate resolutions were needed between October 2010 and April 2011 as part of the Cantor-driven strategy. This also meant there would be multiple threats to shut down portions of the government unless the GOP's demands were met—the equivalent of serial games of chicken, each one with escalating stakes.

Cantor and his House Republicans set hyperambitious goals for cutting spending. They pledged during the campaign and right after the election to cut $100 billion from the 2011 budget. But reality soon set in. With a fiscal year already well under way, cutting $100 billion from the discretionary part of the budget would have meant across-the-board cuts of more than 20 percent, wreaking havoc on programs from homeland security to food safety to disaster relief to air traffic control. The leaders, including Budget Chair Paul Ryan, began backpedaling in January, much to the chagrin—and rage—both of Tea Party freshmen who had made the $100 billion cut a solemn campaign pledge and of more senior conservatives like Jim Jordan of Ohio, chairman of the Republican Study Committee, who wanted even more.

Ryan's heart was with the conservatives, but as Budget Chair, he knew what was practical and achievable in the real world of budgeting. Ryan initially floated a budget plan with cuts barely more than a third of that goal, but with much deeper longer-term reductions. His caucus rebelled, forcing him to go back and double his original cuts. None of the House GOP plans or demands were acceptable to the president or to congressional Democrats. What followed was a set of extended and difficult negotiations between Speaker Boehner, Senate Majority Leader Harry Reid, and President Obama over a continuing resolution, with the date for shutdown looming. Finally, late on Friday, April 8, the leaders announced a deal one hour before the midnight deadline.

That deal made $38 billion in budget cuts for the fiscal year, equal to what even Ryan had said was a feasible—meaning achievable—amount, and adding up to a prorated $78 billion in cuts if taken over the entire year. Boehner boasted that it was "the biggest annual spending cut in history."[9] Even that was not enough to placate all House Republicans; fifty-nine hard-liners, including twenty-seven freshmen, voted against the plan (eighty-one Democrats supported it, enough to enable it to pass). The fact that fifty-nine House Republicans were willing to brush aside Ryan's seal of approval on the numbers was a troubling signal for Boehner's efforts to forge unity in his caucus while trying to achieve the compromises necessary to govern.

But soon after passage of the continuing resolution, more details emerged about the deal, making it clear that the cuts were less than they had appeared on the surface and included a sizable share of budget tricks and legerdemain, with few of the "cuts" actually biting deeply in the short run. Boehner, determined to avoid a debilitating shutdown, had cut a deal that was the best he could do, but one that involved major compromises, cloaked with "budgetese" that would not be deciphered until after the vote. None of the revelations were enough to precipitate a full-scale revolt of rank-and-file conservatives, but the disappointment led many to reinforce their resolve to achieve real and much deeper cuts with the second bite at the apple—the debt limit.

In May, the formal ceiling on the debt of $14.3 trillion was reached, meaning that the clock now started ticking seriously toward a drop-dead date when, without action, the Treasury would not have enough money coming in to pay the bills due each day, from Social Security checks to payments to government contractors or Medicare providers. On Monday, May 2, the stage and its timing were set, as Treasury Secretary Tim Geithner sent a letter to Congress projecting August 2 as the date when Treasury's mechanisms for diverting default, which included borrowing from other accounts, would no longer be available, and the government's receipts would no longer cover its obligations.

The president responded by setting up a series of meetings at Blair House under the direction of Vice President Joe Biden, to try to achieve a compromise and avoid a default. Congressional leaders chose their own representatives for the talks. Congressional Democrats, via House Minority Leader Nancy Pelosi and Senate Majority Leader Harry Reid, sent two representatives each from the House and Senate (House Minority Whip Jim Clyburn and Budget Committee Ranking Member Chris Van Hollen; Senate Appropriations Chair Dan Inouye and Finance Chair Max Baucus). Congressional Republicans, via John Boehner and Mitch McConnell, opted to send only one lawmaker from each house, House Majority Leader Eric Cantor and Senate Minority Whip Jon Kyl. The choices were striking; Democrats Van Hollen, Inouye, and Baucus were known for their deal making; Republicans Cantor and Kyl, for their aversion to deal making. For Speaker Boehner, the choice of Cantor was probably a way to force the latter to be a deal maker, but also a way to legitimize any deal that involved tax increases as part of a compromise with the Tea Party freshmen and the more conservative senior members of his caucus.

The initial session went so well that even Cantor spoke of "good rapport" as the parties discussed spending cuts they could agree on. But the good rapport lasted only for a few weeks. As soon as the issue turned from cutting spending to increasing taxes as a part of a comprehensive plan to cut at least $2 trillion from the long-term debt, the dynamic shifted dramatically. On June 23, Cantor abruptly pulled out of the talks, saying that they would have to break the "impasse" by moving to a higher level, involving the president and the Speaker.

Cantor's move was a sign of his unwillingness to be party to a grand bargain that included taxes, which would undercut his own standing with conservatives. We know now that Cantor's move surprised Speaker Boehner, who reportedly learned of it only moments before it leaked to the press. As *Daily Beast* reporter Patricia Murphy recounted, "After news broke of the majority leader's surprise maneuver, Boehner and Cantor hardly presented a united front. . . . When asked if he had encouraged Cantor to break off the negotiations, Boehner said only that he sympathized with Cantor, clearly distancing himself from his deputy's move." Murphy quoted a Republican aide: "Cantor is basically saying to Boehner, 'Now, it's your problem.'"[10]

If Speaker Boehner had hoped to co-opt his majority leader, it backfired, putting Boehner squarely in the hot seat, while preserving Cantor's purity.

A Grand Bargain?

With Cantor's withdrawal, Boehner was forced to regroup and get directly involved in negotiations. He and President Obama, along with Reid, began intensive negotiations aimed at a "grand bargain," something comparable to what a succession of bipartisan groups had proposed. The goal was to develop a plan reducing projected deficits by $4 trillion over ten years, including restraints on domestic and defense discretionary spending; cutbacks in the growth of Medicare, Medicaid, and Social Security; tax reform to reduce rates and broaden the tax base; and enough revenues to make up the difference.

There were signs that a grand bargain might actually be in the offing, despite the Young Guns and their disciples' reluctance to accept any tax increases. Indeed, Boehner was so bullish about the negotiations that he spoke to the Senate Republican Conference, the caucus of all Senate Republicans, about their progress. But as soon as word emerged that revenues were on the table— the issue that Cantor had said the Speaker would have to resolve—Cantor openly criticized and undercut the negotiations, saying publicly that the House would never pass a plan with tax increases. Again, Boehner was sandbagged. As *Politico*'s David Rogers reported, "Boehner's forces appeared to be shaken Thursday by the skepticism they encountered for even entertaining new tax revenues as part of the package. And the GOP's divisions broke into the open at a White House meeting hosted by Obama for congressional leaders."[11] A few days later, the *Los Angeles Times* quoted a Republican strategist and former leadership aide: "I don't think Boehner would want to serve in a foxhole anytime with Eric Cantor."[12]

By July 9, Boehner was forced to step back from talks of a grand bargain. Though only a few days earlier he had supported it, he now claimed that the White House's insistence on tax hikes meant that only a "smaller bargain," one without taxes and with more limited budget cuts, was feasible. That move put Cantor back into the center of negotiations, and at Boehner's direction, he resumed his role in the discussions. At a White House meeting,

Cantor informed the president and others attending that there wasn't enough time for a deal and that he would call for a short-term extension in the debt ceiling, but one that would only last until the fall, when election season pressure would make it even harder for Republicans, many facing challengers from the Tea Party, to make concessions. An angry Obama responded, "Eric, don't call my bluff," and said that no other president, including Ronald Reagan, would've been willing to sit through such negotiations. He left the room. Soon thereafter, Moody's said it was putting the U.S. on review for a possible downgrade. That warning did not faze Cantor or his followers, who continued to push for deeper spending cuts with no taxes.

Senate Republican Leader Mitch McConnell weighed in on July 13 with his own reflections on why Congress needed to avoid default, not because it would cause serious economic hardship, but because it could damage the Republican brand, just as the blowback from the government shutdown at the end of 1995 had done:

> I refuse to help Barack Obama get re-elected by marching Republicans into a position where we have co-ownership of a bad economy. . . . If we go into default, he will say that Republicans are making the economy worse and try to convince the public—maybe with some merit, if people stop getting their Social Security checks and military families start getting letters saying service people overseas don't get paid. It's an argument he could have a good chance of winning, and all of the sudden we have co-ownership of a bad economy. . . . That is very bad positioning going into an election.[13]

McConnell's statement indicating a desire to cut a deal and avoid default changed the dynamic, but as he said, it was not because he feared the economic consequences for the country, but because the failure to do so would damage the Republican brand. The clear implication was that if default brought economic hardship and the president and Democrats got blamed, that would be just fine. That kind of calculus—putting partisan advantage ahead of problem-solving, with the stakes for the country being sky-high—was not politics as usual, at least not as we have seen it practiced through several generations of party leaders.

The politics and the policy process both changed as August 2 loomed. In the Senate, an informal bipartisan group of six senators, known widely as the Gang of Six, had been meeting since 2009 to try to find a bipartisan debt-reduction plan. It had had its own roller-coaster ride. One of its founders, Tom Coburn of Oklahoma, had walked out of the intensive negotiations in May 2011, saying that his colleagues were not serious about major entitlement reductions, but as the debt limit breach approached, the five remaining members of the gang finally reached a deal on July 19, and Coburn returned belatedly to endorse it. An endorsement also came from Senate Republican Conference Chair Lamar Alexander of Tennessee. Even more notably, President Obama said the plan was "good news" and consistent with his own approach. But, as Mike Allen of *Politico* revealed at the time: "A Senate Republican leadership aide e-mails with subject line 'Gang of Six': 'Background guidance: The President killed any chance of its success by 1) Embracing it. 2) Hailing the fact that it increases taxes. 3) Saying it mirrors his own plan.'"[14]

In other words, anything that Barack Obama is for, Republicans reflexively oppose.

The House Republicans wanted nothing to do with anything that smacked of compromise. Boehner, sensitive to his uneasy position relative to the hard-liners who dominated his ranks, pushed for a vote that took an even harder line, called "Cut, Cap and Balance," which required ten-year statutory spending caps that would cut $5.8 trillion from spending over the decade, where the debt limit increase on the table was for $2.4 trillion. The bill also included a constitutional amendment to balance the budget that would cap spending at 18 percent of GDP, well below recent levels and requiring far more draconian cuts, given population growth and the aging society. Not surprisingly, President Obama said he would veto the bill if sent to him.

David Rogers reported that day:

Washington's frayed nerves showed through Monday amid tough talk on the right, a White House veto threat, canceled weekend passes and the top Senate Democrat likening default to a "very, very scary" outcome even for those "who believe government should be small enough to drown in a bathtub." . . . House Speaker John Boehner confirmed a POLITICO report that he had met again privately with President Obama at the White House on Sunday to try to get the debt talks back on track. But ignoring Obama's veto warning, Boehner will press ahead Tuesday with House votes on a revised debt ceiling bill that shows no signs of compromise on the spending and tax policy differences behind the crisis. . . . [I]n his haste to act, Boehner will bring the so-called Cut, Cap and Balance bill to the floor under exactly the type of procedure he has said he abhors: limited debate and with no real review by any legislative committee.[15]

The bill passed on a nearly party-line vote, 234–190, and was sent to the Senate.

It was subsequently reported that the secret meeting on Sunday, July 17, at the White House that Boehner had confirmed had actually been between Boehner and White House Chief of Staff Bill Daley, along with Treasury Secretary Tim Geithner and OMB Director Jack Lew, with President Obama stopping by on occasion, for intensive negotiations—line by line, some reported—over yet another grand bargain.[16] This deal was to include $800 billion in new revenues through growth and closing loopholes, along with $1.7 trillion in spending cuts, including major changes in entitlements, one of which was to raise the Medicare eligibility age to sixty-seven. The progress over details in the talks suggested that a deal of that magnitude might actually be reached. But many Democrats, leery that the president was not striking a tough enough deal, rebelled. The bipartisan Gang of Six framework actually had more than double the revenue amount in the previous Boehner–White House negotiation (albeit in conjunction with major tax reform). In the eyes of many congressional Democrats, if Obama couldn't get more in revenues, they wanted fewer tough cutbacks in Social Security and Medicare.

The president called Boehner on Thursday afternoon and said that if he were to sign off on the entitlement changes Boehner wanted, the president would need more revenue, perhaps as much as $400 billion more, or the alternative would be to "dial back" on the entitlement cuts. *Time* magazine reporter Jay Newton-Small reported that the president, according to a senior White House aide, told Boehner, "I understand you may not be able to come up on the revenue, and if you can't I'm open to doing something else. . . . We can come down on the revenue and we have to lighten up on the mandatories, the entitlements, a little bit. We can come together on this."[17] The one thing the president said he would not do was succumb to Majority Leader

Cantor's demand that the deal include an end to the individual mandate from the health-care reform act.[18] According to the *Washington Post*'s team of reporters, the president felt the call went well, and that evening he discussed with Democratic congressional leaders the need to accept some tough cuts in Medicare and Medicaid.

But from Thursday night through the next day, Obama's multiple phone calls to Boehner went unreturned. Late Friday afternoon—at exactly 5:31 p.m., too late for the evening news shows—Boehner and the president had an eleven-minute call in which the Speaker told the president he was again walking away from the negotiations. "'At some point,' Obama said, wrapping up his post-collapse press conference the next morning, 'I think if you want to be a leader, then you've got to lead.'"[19]

The near-breakthrough had turned into a highly public breakup. After his conversation with the president—and after the markets had closed for the weekend—Boehner sent a letter to his House Republican colleagues, saying, "A deal was never reached, and was never really close. In the end we couldn't connect. Not because of different personalities, but because of different visions for our country." To those watching the byplay, it seemed clear that a deal had been in sight and Boehner blinked, again fearing a firestorm of criticism from his own colleagues and a lack of backup from the Young Guns in the leadership. Again, he blamed the White House.

The Senate, not surprisingly, rejected the House's "Cut, Cap and Balance" bill on a party line vote on Friday. With barely more than a week until doomsday—and with at least a day or two needed for the Congressional Budget Office to analyze and quantify any deal's budget impact and then turn it into legislative language—the two-day delay caused by the Speaker's failure to return the president's phone call ratcheted up the pressure on Congress. The president called the Speaker and Democratic congressional leaders back to the White House on Saturday morning, again to no avail. On Sunday, Boehner turned up the pressure by suggesting to reporters that he would make a guaranteed vote on a balanced budget constitutional amendment a condition for an increase in the debt limit.

From his perspective, the president had put himself out on a limb to reach a deal, accepting painful changes in Medicare and other entitlements that his party stalwarts passionately opposed, and in return had been openly disrespected by Boehner. He faced the real possibility of a major jolt to an already weak economy; experts predicted that default might send the economy into a deeper tailspin. So he went on national television to offer his own version of what had happened, underscoring his support for the $4 trillion plan he had come close to securing with Boehner. He placed blame not on Boehner but on the other Republicans in Congress who had insisted on a cuts-only approach that Obama chastised as unfair because it spared the wealthy alone any sacrifice. He expressed alarm at the dire consequences, including the first time in history that the nation's AAA credit rating would be downgraded, and decried a six-month extension of the debt limit as irresponsible. He called for compromise and said, "The American people may have voted for divided government but they didn't vote for dysfunctional government."[20]

Boehner followed with his own address from the Capitol to push the Republican narrative: "President Obama came to Congress in January and requested business as usual—yet another routine increase in the debt limit. We in the House said 'not so fast.' . . . What we told the president in January was this: the American people will not accept an increase in the debt limit without significant spending cuts and reforms." He added, "I want you to know I made a sincere effort to work with the president to identify a path forward that would implement the principles of Cut, Cap and Balance in a manner that could secure bipartisan support and be signed into law. I gave it my all. Unfortunately, the president would not take yes for an answer. Even when we thought we might be close to an agreement, the president's demands changed."

With no basis in fact, Boehner went on to say that there was no stalemate in Congress, that he believed a bill close to his latest version of "Cut, Cap and Balance," which only raised the debt limit by $900 billion, leaving another showdown before the 2012 election, would pass the Senate and avert the crisis—after the Senate finished debating its own bill "filled with phony accounting and Washington gimmicks." Boehner's optimism about Senate reaction to his plan received a blow on July 27, when every Senate Democrat signed a letter declaring opposition to the Boehner package. And it also came under siege from his own House conservatives, with Jim Jordan of Ohio saying that he was confident that there were not 218 Republicans in support of their Speaker's plan.

Boehner delayed the vote as he negotiated with his conservatives, changing the plan in a rightward direction so, for example, it required that a constitutional amendment to balance the budget not just be brought to a vote but actually *pass* through Congress and be sent to the states. The bill authorized $900 billion in borrowing while reducing spending by $917 billion over ten years. It enabled the president to request a second increase in borrowing of up to $1.6 trillion, conditioned on passage in both houses (by a two-thirds vote) of the balanced budget constitutional amendment and passage of a separate $1.8 trillion deficit-reduction plan. By moving his bill even more sharply to the right, Boehner and his lieutenants scored just enough votes to pass the plan on Friday, July 29, even as the Senate voted 59 to 41 to table a resolution to bring the plan forward in the upper chamber. The vote in the House was 218–210. Twenty-two Republicans voted against the bill, and no Democrats supported it.

The House and Senate continued to play their game of chicken, but over the next two days, Obama, Boehner, and McConnell, along with Reid, continued to negotiate as the clock ticked toward the deadline. They finally reached an agreement late Sunday, July 31, in just enough time to have it passed and enacted before budgetary Armageddon hit. The complex deal included no tax increases, but extended the debt limit adequately—assuming no serious additional economic downturn—to get through the election, with deficit reduction coming in two tranches. The first tranche was $900 billion, requiring offsetting cuts in discretionary spending over ten years, with $400 billion of them immediate to avert default. That would be followed by an additional $1.2 trillion to $1.5 trillion increase in the limit, with a new "super committee" of twelve, evenly divided by party and chamber, to recommend offsetting debt reductions that would receive guaranteed, up-or-down votes in both houses. If the committee could not attain a majority, or if Congress rejected the committee plan, a set of across-the-board cuts, coming equally from defense and other programs, with a small portion from Medicare, would be triggered.

While both liberal Democrats and conservative Republicans criticized the plan, it managed to make it comfortably through the House and Senate on Monday, in time to avert the worst. The vote in the House was 269–161; 174 Republicans joined 95 Democrats in favor, and 66 Republicans and 95 Democrats voted no. In the Senate, the vote was 74 to 26. The nays included 19 Republicans and 7 Democrats.

Relieved congressional leaders were in a self-congratulatory mood after the votes. Not many other people or institutions were. The markets reacted badly, in part because most economists and investors believed that the already weakened economy would be further damaged by the root canal of immediate spending cuts. And despite the deal, Standard & Poor's downgraded the United States four days later, blaming, as we noted at the beginning of this chapter, the dysfunctional political process. In previous "Perils of Pauline" style episodes of brinksmanship on the debt limit, the U.S. never came close to a downgrade, suggesting again how different and more destructive the politics had become.

"A Hostage Worth Ransoming"

Mitch McConnell continued to be astonishingly candid about his view that the permanent campaign had trumped policy, with analysis that suggested that this was a perfectly acceptable course, meaning many more upheavals to come. He said, "I think some of our members may have thought the default issue was a hostage you might take a chance at shooting. Most of us didn't think that. *What we did learn is this—it's a hostage worth ransoming*."[21] McConnell went further the day after the Senate vote, in an interview with Fox News's Neil Cavuto:

It set the template for the future. In the future, Neil, no president—in the near future, maybe in the distant future— is going to be able to get the debt ceiling increased without a re-ignition of the same discussion of how do we cut spending and get America headed in the right direction. I expect the next president, whoever that is, is going to be asking us to raise the debt ceiling again in 2013, *so we'll be doing it all over.*[22]

House Majority Whip Kevin McCarthy was especially proud of the role the intransigent freshmen and other arch conservatives had played; the genuine threat that they would take the country down via default, he said, forced Democrats to accept an unpalatable deal. As the *Washington Post* reporters noted, Jason Chaffetz, "who voted against both Boehner's first proposal and the final bill, said he was well aware of how the leadership had used his and others' willingness to let a default happen as a negotiating chip, and said he didn't mind at all. *'We weren't kidding around, either,'* he said. *'We would have taken it down.'*"[23]

It is of course possible that the willingness of bomb-throwing rank-and-file lawmakers to bring the system crashing down, and the eagerness of cold-blooded congressional leaders to hold the nation's full faith and credit for ransom on a now-regular basis, will lead ultimately to positive policy outcomes, though that was nowhere evident when the dust settled in 2011. The whole dynamic of the debt ceiling battle that poisoned the well in Washington left more than a disgruntled ratings agency and a dissatisfied chairman of the Federal Reserve.

To us, the battle was a template for all that is wrong with contemporary society and politics. Balancing interests, conducting meaningful deliberation and debate, respecting adversaries and, most of all, focusing on problem solving all took a backseat to the Republicans' take-it-or-leave-it bargaining positions. Many shrill voices on talk radio, cable television, blogs, and Twitter urged on the most intransigent of forces; they were joined in an unprecedented way by ostensibly credible opinion leaders, including senators like Pat Toomey of Pennsylvania, presidential candidates like Tim Pawlenty, billionaire investors like Stanley Druckenmiller, and a slew of serious commentators providing reassurance that default was no big deal.[24]

The typical voices of caution and prudence were drowned out by the take-no-prisoners crowd. The idea that immediate deep budget cuts could weaken the slow economic recovery, possibly creating a double-dip recession, was ignored. There is no avoiding the fact that this crowd was located on the Republican side of the aisle. With a Democratic president, the opponents of a debt ceiling deal were naturally going to be concentrated on the GOP side—but the intensity of support for actual default was not routine.

Not surprisingly, the public was appalled by the entire spectacle and overwhelmingly unimpressed with the outcome. Ratings of the Congress and the president, as well as confidence in the ability of the government to improve the grave economic conditions, dropped even further. A problem precipitated by one party's deliberate intransigence caused damage to all the actors in the process, suggesting that any real accountability for bad behavior would be elusive.

The deal that was reached did offer a new opening for sanity, with the creation of the super committee—technically, the Joint Select Committee on Deficit Reduction—to take the bold steps toward a ten-year plan that would stabilize the federal debt-to-GDP ratio (the size of debt relative to the overall economy), authorize additional short-term stimulus to boost the tepid recovery, and begin to lower the shocking level of unemployment. In blunt terms, the super committee was designed to transcend the dysfunction and get to "yes," to the ten-year, $4 trillion debt-reduction plan that we described earlier—based on the common template shaped by various outside commissions (the presidential one known as Simpson-Bowles and one created by the Bipartisan Policy Center known as Rivlin-Domenici) and the one informal inside group (the Senate "Gang of Six") that had previously tackled the problem. By giving the committee unprecedented leverage—both houses would vote on any product without delay or amendment—the president and congressional leaders had at least offered a way out. And the congressional leaders appointed some members, like Republican Senator Rob Portman of Ohio and Representative Dave Camp of Michigan, and Democratic Senator John Kerry and Representative Chris Van Hollen, who were all knowledgeable and inclined to make deals.

But in the end, dysfunction driven by tribalism would win again. Republican opposition to significant revenue increases, which had torpedoed earlier negotiations between Obama and Boehner, remained the dominant stumbling block. Nothing fundamental had changed. Early on, Democrats on the committee, to the dismay of many liberals in and out of Congress, offered significant concessions on sensitive entitlements like Medicare, in return for sufficient revenues to make a balanced package in line with the ones crafted by Simpson-Bowles and Rivlin-Domenici. True, the Democrats did not get into specific details, leaving those to negotiations. But there was a long period without relevant negotiation because the Republicans on the committee refused to consider any tax increases as part of the package. Toward the deadline of November 23, 2011, negotiations evolved into a semblance of give-and-take, as the strong anti-tax Senator Pat Toomey offered approximately $300 billion in revenue increases. That sounded promising, but there was a condition—that Democrats agree to the permanent extension of all the Bush tax cuts otherwise scheduled to expire at the end of 2012, at a cost of $3.7 trillion in lost revenue. Toomey's insistence that the maximum marginal tax rate be lowered well below the Bush levels made the offer even worse, meaning an even greater loss of revenue. That made the offer a non-starter. Despite the fact that forty-five senators and a hundred House members from across the partisan and ideological spectrums called for the grand bargain, it was not to be.

The presumed Republican deal makers put party fealty ahead of problem solving, showing that near-religious anti-tax cant continues to rule. One reason: As 145 members of Congress called for a bipartisan bargain, 70 House Republicans, led by fire-breather Patrick McHenry of North Carolina insisted that there be not a dime of tax increases. They joined other conservative activists who denounced even the Toomey offer—a net tax cut of well over $3 trillion—as off-limits because it used the words *tax* and *increase* together. Despite the fact that a majority of Americans, including a majority of Republicans, supported a broad deficit deal including increased taxes on the rich, the super committee Republicans, presumably along with the leaders who chose them, sided with the fringe ideological base. What better example of deep dysfunction?

The failure to reach an agreement left in place the first tranche of spending cuts approved as part of the debt ceiling deal that created the super committee as well as automatic cuts that are to begin in January 2013. These spending reductions are not directed at the main drivers of the projected deficits—health-care cost increases and inadequate revenues—and could well inflict substantial damage on the wellsprings of future economic growth and national security.

In 2010, an angry and frightened electorate had put the Republicans in the majority in the House and strengthened the GOP's hand in the Senate. What that produced was a year of hostage taking and wrangling in Congress, misdirected steps to deal with the deficit, and nothing whatsoever to remedy the public's greatest concern—chronic unemployment. Democracy's most essential power—the ability of the citizenry to "throw the bums out"—proved wholly inadequate to the task of governing effectively.

The Seeds of Dysfunction

The current climate of broken politics goes well beyond issues like the debt limit and spending. The problems are much deeper and broader, inside Congress, in the relations between Congress and the president, in campaigns, and in the coarsened, divided, and tribal political culture. But the problems did not emerge overnight. Some of their roots go back to major societal shifts in the 1960s; others are far more recent. But as we witnessed ourselves, none of the roots have been more important than developments set in motion in the election of 1978.

Newt Gingrich's Mark on American Politics

In 1978, the two of us formed an affiliation with the American Enterprise Institute (AEI) to create an entity we called "The Congress Project" to track Congress as an institution through an era of change. During the previous decade, both the House and

Senate had undergone significant reforms in their internal rules and procedures, opening things up to more public scrutiny and to a role for more rank-and-file members as the seniority system was shaken. New-style members less tied to the status quo were elected, new politics were evident in campaigns and the country, and Congress was evolving in ways that demanded serious analysis.

We started the Congress Project in the midst of the 1978 midterm campaign—a seminal one, as it turned out. A group called the National Conservative Political Action Committee, or NCPAC, founded three years earlier by activists John Terry Dolan, Charles Black, and Roger Stone, emerged as a major force in the campaign, financing an independent spending campaign against liberal Democrats like Senators Dick Clark of Iowa and Tom McIntyre of New Hampshire. NCPAC produced a barrage of negative ads and passed out flyers at places like churches in an effort that ultimately brought down both candidates. One memorable flyer accused Clark, a supporter of abortion rights, of being a baby killer. By today's standards, NCPAC's campaigns were comparatively mild, but they were significant as the first example of what would soon become common on both ends of the political spectrum: nationalized, highly ideological, independent-expenditure campaigns.

Our first program at AEI recruited a small group of the freshman representatives that year to participate in regular, off-the-record dinners during their first term in the House. The idea was to allow them to talk candidly about their immersion in the legislative process and the political dynamics of the House. We sought members who would in some ways be representative of the body, but who also had potential, based on their backgrounds and campaigns, to be serious players in the years ahead. Among that group were Newt Gingrich, Dick Cheney, and Geraldine

Ferraro. From the first session, it was Gingrich, a history professor at a small Georgia college who had twice run unsuccessfully for the House before he finally won, who stood out among the rest for his self-assurance and strategy, already fully articulated, for achieving a Republican majority in the House.[1]

Though he came to be viewed as a quintessential "movement conservative"—and that is the way he characterized himself during his 2012 presidential run—in those days Gingrich was much more flexible than ideologically rigid. He supported increased government funding in areas where he had a strong personal affinity, like science and health research. The Democrats had controlled the House that Gingrich entered for twenty-four years, and he believed that the great advantages conferred by incumbent status made a race-by-race approach to winning a majority for his party a losing one. How, Gingrich wondered, could the minority party overcome the seemingly paradoxical situation in which people hated the Congress but loved their own congressman?[2] The strategy he settled on would bring him to power but have a devastating impact on the institution he ultimately led.

What was Gingrich's strategy? He was both passionate about his goals and coldly analytical in his means. The core strategy was to destroy the institution in order to save it, to so intensify public hatred of Congress that voters would buy into the notion of the need for sweeping change and throw the majority bums out. His method? To unite his Republicans in refusing to cooperate with Democrats in committee and on the floor, while publicly attacking them as a permanent majority presiding over and benefiting from a thoroughly corrupt institution. Most of Gingrich's colleagues in our dinner group, both Democrats and Republicans, were deeply unsettled by his description of that strategy, a sentiment many of his fellow Republicans shared over the next several years. One exception: Dick Cheney, an establishment Republican who quickly moved up in leadership ranks in the House, but who sympathized with Gingrich and his approach, and developed an enduring friendship with him.

After Ronald Reagan was elected president in 1980, the ranks of Gingrich's insurgents were reinforced, opening the door for him to form the Conservative Opportunity Society (COS), an informal group of frustrated minority lawmakers. They set out to create an alternative power structure to that of Minority Leader Bob Michel of Illinois, who had worked well with his counterpart, Speaker Thomas P. O'Neill. COS was abetted by a Democratic majority that had grown complacent and arrogant. In a proto-insurgency movement, COS and its supporters used politically motivated amendments and overheated, hyperbolic rhetoric to poke and agitate Democratic leaders. They responded, as Gingrich anticipated, by overreacting, shutting off Republican amendments, and using or misusing the gavel to avoid embarrassing votes. Along the way, they radicalized even moderate Republicans who had been content to work within the system as minor partners.

Perhaps the seminal moment of this campaign of agitation came in the spring of 1984. In the back story, the House had a tradition of "special orders," evening hours after the official business was done when members could reserve time to read speeches that would appear in the Congressional Record, even though they generally delivered them to an empty chamber. Usually, these speeches involved mundane and relatively unimportant things, such as allowing lawmakers to praise constituents. But the potential for political exploitation of evening hours changed markedly in March 1979, just three months after Gingrich took office, when C-SPAN launched its gavel-to-gavel coverage of House proceedings. Under House rules, cameras were put in fixed positions trained on speakers, with no camera operators panning the chamber. Ironically, the rules were intended to *prevent* political exploitation of the televised proceedings.

What Gingrich realized was that the fixed cameras meant C-SPAN viewers had no idea the speakers in the evening sessions were in fact addressing empty seats in the chamber. Although the C-SPAN audiences were not enormous, it was still an opportunity to reach the most politically involved voters. Gingrich and his allies began a regular process of reserving time in the evening, and a small group of lawmakers engaged in colloquies that attacked Democrats for opposing school prayer, being soft on Communism, and being corrupt. Gingrich called Democrats "blind to communism" and threatened to file charges against ten Democrats who had sent a warm letter to Nicaraguan leftist leader Daniel Ortega. In the favored technique, the lawmaker speaking turned as if he were addressing Democrats in the chamber, and the lack of response made it appear as if those in the audience either accepted the charges or were unwilling or unable to counter them.

This procedure went on for months, and in early May 1984, Speaker O'Neill decided it was time to retaliate by ordering C-SPAN cameras to pan the chamber during these special orders, showing the empty seats in the chamber. O'Neill also attacked Gingrich for impugning the patriotism of Democrats. On May 14, Gingrich took to the floor of the House and, with O'Neill in the chair, accused the Speaker not only of violating the rules, but of using words that came "all too close to resembling a McCarthyism of the Left."

A *Los Angeles Times* reporter recounted what followed:

> [T]he venerable Speaker exploded. "You deliberately stood in that well before an empty House, and challenged

these people, and challenged their patriotism," O'Neill thundered, "and it is the lowest thing that I've seen in my 32 years in Congress." Gingrich's predecessor as whip, Rep. Trent Lott (R-Miss.) immediately sprang from his seat. In the supposedly decorous House, members are barred from launching personal attacks against one another on the floor, a rule about which Gingrich had pirouetted with near-gymnastic skill. The presiding officer had no choice and ruled in Lott's favor. The confrontation with O'Neill was big news, and Gingrich announced, "I am now a famous person."[3]

That episode added to Democrats' rage, which in turn led them to clamp down harder on Republicans, creating even more partisan hard feelings. The explosion with O'Neill was no accident. In a 1984 profile of Gingrich, a veteran reporter wrote:

I watched him [Gingrich] give a speech to a group of conservative activists. "The number one fact about the news media," he told them, "is they love fights." For months, he explained, he had been giving "organized, systematic, researched, one-hour lectures. Did CBS rush in and ask if they could tape one of my one-hour lectures? No. But the minute Tip O'Neill attacked me, he and I got 90 seconds at the close of all three network news shows. You have to give them confrontations. When you give them confrontations, you get attention; when you get attention, you can educate."[4]

Gingrich wasn't done. In 1988, he attacked O'Neill's successor, Jim Wright, with a relentless barrage of ethics charges, mostly based on newspaper reports that Wright had improper associations with savings and loan officials and other business leaders. Initially, the House brushed the charges aside, until another event triggered a new populist explosion that put Wright and the majority Democrats in the House largely on the defensive. In 1989, members of Congress voted a substantial pay raise for themselves and other top officials. This vote was the result of a broad bipartisan leadership agreement, with support from outgoing President Reagan, incoming President George H. W. Bush, and congressional leaders of both parties, including Gingrich (who soon after Bush ascended to the presidency had been elected House Minority Whip to replace Dick Cheney). The result was a firestorm of criticism largely directed at the Democratic leadership and Speaker Wright, already tainted by the ethics charges. Although Gingrich had supported the pay raise, that fact did not stop him from turning on Wright and the Democrats, blaming the majority for the pay raise decision.

Shortly after the pay raise, the Democrats experienced the full fury of the populist reaction. Arriving in a group at Washington's Union Station, bound for their annual party retreat at the Greenbrier, a resort in West Virginia, they were met by a crowd of protestors angrily denouncing the pay raise. Many House Democrats, feeling under siege, huddled together on the train ride blaming Wright, who they viewed as having done nothing to counter the attacks, for their plight. When the entourage arrived at the Greenbrier, they found network news reporters set up on the lawn, doing their stand-up reports from "the posh Greenbrier resort," the worst possible image for embattled lawmakers.

Wright had lost support of his own party, and before the year was out, the House ethics committee charged him with a series of relatively minor offenses, including improper bulk sales of his book to interest groups seeking his favor. If in an earlier era the result would have been a reprimand, in this atmosphere there was no way Wright could stay as Speaker without irreparable damage to his party and the House. He resigned on May 31, 1989, further reinforcing the public's image of Congress as corrupt. Wright's farewell address from the House floor decried what he called the "mindless cannibalism" that had overtaken Congress, referring not so subtly to the campaign against him led by Newt Gingrich.

A new and vastly exaggerated media focus on a fat and perk-laden Congress filled with members living luxurious lives got new traction with a scandal in 1992 over the House bank. For many decades, the House had maintained an internal bank that deposited members' paychecks temporarily until they were transferred to other accounts. Lawmakers could draw against their pay via House bank checks, and many had multiple overdrafts. Since the only money in the bank was from the pay of all lawmakers, the overdrafts were not misusing taxpayer money, but the idea that members of Congress could overdraw their accounts in ways that average voters could not caused further outrage. Ironically, that Gingrich himself had twenty-two overdrafts didn't seem to matter.[5]

A group of Gingrich allies calling themselves the "Gang of Seven" seized on the bank scandal to take Gingrich's confrontational tactics to new levels. Its ringleaders were Rick Santorum of Pennsylvania; John Boehner of Ohio, then only in his second year as a member; and Jim Nussle of Iowa. Their most memorable moment came when Nussle put a brown paper bag over his head while on the House floor, proclaiming that he was ashamed to be a member of Congress. The C-SPAN footage was repeated over and over on network newscasts. Gingrich's goal of causing voters to feel enough disgust at the entire Congress that they would throw out the majority was within reach; he attained it a little more than two years later.

In 1992, the electorate, reacting to a poor economy, brought in a Democratic president for the first time in twelve years, with continuing Democratic majorities in both houses of Congress. This scenario was ideal for Gingrich, as it allowed him to capitalize on his party's frustration at being out of power at both ends of Pennsylvania Avenue for the first time in twelve years; he was able to convince his party to vote en masse against major Clinton initiatives. Gingrich in effect convinced Republicans to act like a parliamentary minority; even in areas where some GOP members might have agreed with Democrats or wanted to bargain with them, they united in opposition, daring the majority to find votes only from within their own ranks. When Clinton could not keep the congressional Democrats united, it resulted in embarrassing and damaging policy delays and, on his signature health-care reform plan, spectacular failure, along with a deepening sense among voters of a broken political system. That sense was just what Gingrich and his allies wanted to cultivate.

As the 1994 midterm elections approached, Gingrich toured the country recruiting congressional candidates to run against incumbent Democrats and to pursue relentlessly the charge that Congress was corrupt and needed to be blown up to change things. He provided candidates with speeches and language echoing his own themes of rampant corruption in Washington and a House rotten to the core. This tactic included a memo that instructed them to use certain words when talking about the Democratic enemy: *betray, bizarre, decay, anti-flag, anti-family, pathetic, lie, cheat, radical, sick, traitors*, and more.[6] It worked more spectacularly than he could have imagined. The midterm brought huge Republican gains—fifty-two seats—and its first majority in the House in forty years. Following the resignation of Republican Minority Leader Bob Michel, Gingrich, the Republican Whip and universally acknowledged heir apparent, was elected Speaker of the House. It had taken Gingrich sixteen years to realize his objective of a House Republican majority, but his original strategy to gain power by attacking his adversaries and delegitimizing the Congress left a lasting mark on American politics.

The seventy-three freshmen in the class of 1994, nearly a third of the Republican majority, were strong Gingrich loyalists who not only shared his disdain for Congress as an institution but believed it more deeply than he did, and who added their own conservative populist distrust of leaders and leadership. Freshman gadflies like Joe Scarborough of Florida, J. D. Hayworth of Arizona, Helen Chenoweth of Idaho, and Mark Neumann of Wisconsin were fiery and uncompromising. Scarborough and John Shadegg of Arizona, along with a handful of allies, sharply chastised Gingrich for liking earmarks and big spending; Gingrich in return called them "jihadists."[7] Neumann, the only freshman appointed to the Appropriations Committee, insisted on bucking the leaders and promoting his own budget, while voting regularly against the committee leaders. (In 1997, he committed party apostasy by voting "present" for Speaker, meaning he was openly refusing to cast his ballot for Gingrich.) At the urging of Gingrich and other leaders, most left their families in their districts and spent as little time in Washington as possible. Some, like Mark Sanford of South Carolina, eschewed a Washington residence and slept in their offices, as a mark of their determination not to be captured by the evil Capitol culture.

Gingrich wanted to establish the House almost as a parallel government, challenging the president and his policy initiatives— and his very ability to shape the agenda—at every turn. Believing that Clinton was soft and would cave to pressure, enabling the House Republicans to move from winning an election for Congress to taking effective charge of the government and implementing a sweeping policy revolution, he confronted Clinton and challenged established policies at every turn. Most of his efforts centered on issues in the Contract with America, the conservative pledge he and Republican candidates had run on in the 1994 election, that included elements like a balanced budget amendment, a tough crime package, and term limits for members of Congress. The business community, which had benefited from clean air rules, repelled his early attempt to erase existing environmental regulations.

Most of the congressional challenge to Clinton came over budget-related matters, as the House Republicans tried to use the threat of a breach in the debt limit and of shutdowns in major parts of the government to bludgeon the president into accepting their demands to cut spending and cut regulations and taxes. A series of threats and confrontations culminated at the end of the Speaker's first year in two government shutdowns, which backfired on Gingrich and his party. To his credit, Gingrich saw that his overreach and hubris threatened his majority's ability to win a second term; he was still popular enough to convince his colleagues to pivot and work with the president and to have sufficient accomplishments to mollify voters, even if it meant burnishing Clinton's status at the same time.

A new, if brief, period of bipartisan cooperation followed in 1996 on welfare and modest health reform that helped Clinton win reelection and Gingrich to lead his party to a second consecutive term in the majority, albeit with a smaller margin. But the bitterness and rancor he had triggered in his time in the minority blew back against him as he approached his second term as speaker. Democrats brought a slew of ethics charges against Gingrich, including some stunningly similar to the charges that Gingrich had brought against Jim Wright nine years earlier. His speakership hung in the balance, but unlike Wright, he managed to hold on, in a deal that included a reprimand by the House for claiming tax-exempt status for a college course that was used for political purposes, and for repeatedly misleading the House and its ethics investigators, and a $300,000 fine.

Two years later, it was a different matter. His reign as Speaker, which had been both consequential and troubled, ended ignominiously in the heat of the Republican effort to impeach President Clinton. In spite of strong public sentiment against forcing Clinton from office for his misbehavior in the Monica Lewinsky affair, Gingrich orchestrated a last-minute advertising blitz to make the impeachment debate an electoral liability for the Democrats in the 1998 midterm elections. The effort backfired, the Democrats won five seats (reversing the historic pattern of midterm seat losses by the president's party), and pressure built within his party caucus for Gingrich to resign.

Gingrich left with barely a whimper, but remained a visible figure in both political and policy circles by building an extensive network of advocacy organizations. By the time he ran for president in 2011, he had evolved fully from the pragmatic, relatively nonideological though intensely ambitious new member of Congress who first plotted to take majority control of the Congress, to what now passes for a conventional right-wing populist, abandoning long-held positions on health-care reform and cap-and-trade, for example, to cater to the new Tea Party–driven forces that have co-opted the GOP.

Gingrich deserves a dubious kind of credit for many of the elements that have produced the current state of politics. He crystalized the approach of crafting a cohesive, parliamentary-style minority party and using it as a battering ram to stymie and damage a president of the other party. By moving to paint with a broad brush his own institution as elitist, corrupt, and arrogant, he undermined basic public trust in Congress and government, reducing the institution's credibility over a long period. His attacks on partisan adversaries in the White House and Congress created a norm in which colleagues with different views became mortal enemies. In nationalizing congressional elections, he helped invent the modern permanent campaign, allowing electoral goals to dominate policy ones; the use of overheated rhetoric and ethics charges as political weapons; and the take-no-prisoner politics of confrontation and obstruction that have become the new normal. Many members of the House freshman class of 1994, and others who were Gingrich allies like Rick Santorum, ultimately moved to the Senate, taking the norms they had inculcated in the House to the previously more restrained Senate and helping to move its culture in a more confrontational and obstructive direction.[8]

Of course, the dynamic was not entirely one-sided. The tit-for-tat exchanges on ethics cut both ways. If Gingrich had mastered the extensive use of character assaults for political ends, the Democrats took the confrontation over judicial nominations to a new level with their brutal attacks on Robert Bork in 1987. This in turn enraged conservatives nationally and particularly in the Senate, leading to an endless cycle of confrontation over judicial nominees.[9] But one has to look back to Gingrich as the singular political figure who set the tone that followed.

Deeper Roots: The Development of the Divide

If Gingrich and his allies set the table for today's dysfunction, with more than a dollop of help from his adversaries, they were not operating in a vacuum. The seeds of the partisan divide had been planted much earlier, and its roots are deep and strong.

Partisan polarization is undeniably the central and most problematic feature of contemporary American politics. Political parties today are more internally unified and ideologically distinctive than they have been in over a century. This pattern is most evident in the Congress, state legislatures, and other bastions of elite politics, where the ideological divide is wide and where deep and abiding partisan conflict is the norm. But it also reaches the activist stratum of the parties and into the arena of mass politics, as voters increasingly sort themselves by ideology into either the Democratic or Republican Party and view politicians, public issues, and even facts and objective conditions through distinctly partisan lenses.

The Ideological Schism

Scholars have amply measured and established the sharp increase in polarization over the last three decades. We can see it in roll call voting patterns in the House and Senate. As Figure 2-1[10] shows, the period from the end of Reconstruction through the first decade of the twentieth century was also a deeply partisan one, reflecting divisions on issues like farming and whether the United States should rely on the gold or silver standard for its money. Earlier periods in American history also experienced sharp partisan conflict—from battles over federalism in the early decades of the republic to slavery in the 1850s.[11] But for most of the past century, the parties were less internally unified and ideologically distinctive, and more coalitions in Congress cut across parties than is the case today. All the evidence on parties in government in recent years points to very high unity within and sharp ideological and policy differences between the two major

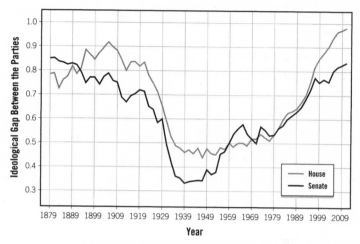

Figure 2-1 Party Polarization, 1879–2010:
Ideological Gap Between the Parties.

parties. As *National Journal* reported in its study of roll call voting in the 111th Congress, for the first time in modern history, in both the House and Senate, the most conservative Democrat is slightly more liberal than the most liberal Republican. This is another way of saying that the degree of overlap between the parties in Congress is zero.[12]

Similar patterns are apparent among party activists of all sorts—delegates to national party conventions, local opinion leaders, issue advocates, donors, and participants in nominating caucuses and primaries. All increasingly share the ideological perspective and issue positions of their party's elected officials.[13]

Contrary to the impression left by many stories in the press, members of the public have also been caught up in partisan polarization, although this varies a good deal by their degree of attachment to one of the parties, their level of information about politics and public affairs, and whether they vote. The general public surely remains less interested and engaged in public affairs, less ideological, and more instinctively pragmatic and open to compromise than the political class.[14] Hot-button social issues of transcendent importance to activists, such as abortion and same-sex marriage, seldom register high on the list of priorities for the broad public. The style and tone of partisan debate is often unsettling to ordinary citizens. But as a number of scholars have demonstrated,[15] critical segments of the general public have been pulled in the same directions as political elites. Voters are more ideologically polarized than nonvoters. More educated, informed, and engaged voters are more polarized than less educated, informed, and engaged voters. Those voters who identify themselves as independents without leaning toward one of the parties (less than 10 percent of the electorate) are mostly bereft of any ideological framework or well-defined issue positions, unlike those who identify or lean toward a party. But active and engaged Democrats and Republicans view the political world through such sharply different lenses—with different perceptions of reality—that their worldviews reinforce the polarization of their elected representatives.

What caused the party polarization? It would be nice if we could boil it down to a single root cause. The pundits' favorite cause, in spite of impressive evidence to the contrary,[16] is the gerrymandering of legislative districts. Redistricting does matter somewhat. It contributes to party polarization by systematically shaping more safe districts for each party, thereby helping to create homogeneous echo chambers, to make party primaries the only real threat to representatives, and to enhance the power of the small number of activist ideologues who dominate in primaries. But that impact is relatively minor and marginal. A recounting of recent history (buttressed by a good deal of scholarly research) reveals that polarization has multiple roots and that those roots are entwined and run deep.[17]

The story begins with the fissures in the Democratic Party's New Deal coalition that were evident in the 1960s, with an initial weakening of the party's stronghold in the South, the rise of the counterculture, and opposition to the war in Vietnam. The 1964 presidential campaign of Barry Goldwater initiated a long-term struggle among Republican activists to develop a more distinctly conservative party agenda. While Goldwater got trounced in the election, he did win (in addition to his home state of Arizona) five Southern states, aided by his outspoken support of states' rights. The five states included Alabama, Mississippi, and South Carolina for the first Republican victory since Reconstruction, and Georgia for the first time *ever*.

This was followed by the passage of the Voting Rights Act of 1965, which, along with the ongoing economic development in the South, began to break the hegemony of conservative whites that had allowed the Democrats to dominate the region for many decades. The Supreme Court's 1973 abortion decision in *Roe v. Wade* galvanized a pro-life movement that years later would form the core of the Republican Party's largest and most reliable constituency, the religious conservatives. California's tax-limiting Proposition 13 in 1978 and the emergence of Ronald Reagan on the national political scene gave the Republican Party a more distinctive economic platform. As president, Reagan vigorously challenged the Soviet Union, adding national security to the set of issues dividing the parties.

Party realignment in the South—fueled by the developments associated with race, religious fundamentalism, economic development, and patriotism—led to a sharp decline in the number of conservative Democrats serving in Congress and an increase in the number of conservative Republicans. In 1980, conservative Democrats made up at least a third of the party; the numbers regularly declined, until they reached roughly 10 percent of the party in 2011. At the same time, the remaining Southern Democrats consisted largely of liberals (mostly minorities). The shift was accelerated by the redistricting coalitions that developed between Republicans and African Americans eager to increase their numbers in Congress by creating majority-minority districts. For Republicans, this meant "packing" Democrats into safe urban districts, giving the GOP more opportunities to win swing suburban seats, while minorities got more representation in districts that had substantial majorities of African-American voters. Those forces alone accounted for most of the increased ideological polarization between the parties in Congress.

The change in the South was enhanced as well by changing migration patterns, as more senior citizens moved to the Sunbelt from colder climes. The late congressional scholar Nelson Polsby noted that the increase in air conditioning, which meant that people could tolerate the oppressive summers in the South, enhanced this trend.[18] As Republican-oriented senior citizens, who came of age before the New Deal, moved South, the regions they left, including New England and the rest of the Northeast, lost a sizable portion of their Republican voting base, endangering the mostly moderate and liberal Republicans who had historically won in those areas.

Parallel changes occurred on the West Coast, which had been a bastion of moderate Republicanism via lawmakers like Mark Hatfield of Oregon and Tom Kuchel of California. But the movement of Asians and Mexican Americans into states like California, Washington, and Oregon, along with others who were drawn to the environmentally conscious and socially moderate atmosphere on the West Coast, turned those states from the 1960s through the 1980s into reliably Democratic strongholds, even as they contributed to the demise of moderate Republicans in Congress.

As these developments played out over time, Democrats in Congress became more homogeneous and drifted left, Republicans became more homogeneous and veered sharply right, and party platforms became more distinctive. The realigning process initiated in the South and then extended to the rest of the country was further fueled by the increasingly distinctive positions that the national parties and their presidential candidates took on a number of salient social and economic issues. Those recruited to Congress (or motivated to run on their own) were more ideologically in tune with their fellow partisans, congressional leaders were given the authority to aggressively promote their party's agenda and message, interest groups increasingly aligned themselves with one party or the other, network news lost audience share and was challenged by more partisan cable news and talk radio, and voters across the country gradually adjusted their party attachments to fit their ideological views.[19]

At the same time, voters were making residential decisions that reinforced the ideological sorting already under way.[20] Citizens were drawn to neighborhoods, counties, states, and regions where others shared their values and interests. This ideological sorting, geographic mobility, and more consistent party-line voting produced many areas that were dominated by a single party at the municipal, county, and state levels, and in state legislative and congressional districts. Contrary to then Illinois state senator Barack Obama's demurral at the 2004 National Democratic Convention in Boston, the portrait of a red and blue nation had some considerable basis in reality. In turn, the increasing partisan homogeneity of political jurisdictions, exacerbated in legislative districts by redistricting practices, diminished electoral competition and reinforced the polarizing dynamic between political elites and voters.

There is another element in this dynamic that has contributed mightily to the amplification of dysfunction—the fact that 1994 brought with it not just the first Republican House in forty years, but also a new era of toss-up elections with party control at stake. Polarized parties raised the stakes of each election by enlarging the consequences of a change in party control. If there had been a shift in party control when we first came to Washington in 1969, it would have meant a move from one figurative forty-yard line to the other. Now it means a move from one goalpost to the opposite twenty-five yard line, or vice versa.

The Republican Party, especially after taking the majority in 1995, honed its political machine to boost both electoral and legislative prospects. Both parties, seeing higher stakes, changed their fund-raising strategies to put a high priority on redistributing resources from the many safe districts to the few remaining competitive ones, effectively involving all members in the larger campaign to retain or achieve majority status. Regular order in the legislative process—the set of rules, practices, and norms designed to ensure a reasonable level of deliberation and fair play in committee, on the floor, and in conference—was often sacrificed for political expediency.[21] That meant, among other things, constraining debates and amendments, and the virtual demise of the conference committees traditionally used to work out the differences between the House and Senate to allow leaders to shape bills behind closed doors. The most egregious case remains the outrageous three-hour vote in 2003 in the wee hours of the morning, violating numerous House rules and norms, to pass the Medicare prescription drug bill.

The election in 2000 of the first unified Republican government since 1952—but with the president elected by a minority of popular votes in the most controversial election in more than a century, a fifty-fifty Senate, a slender majority in the House, and efforts to jam through serious policy on party lines—further hardened party divisions in Congress. The return of a unified Democratic government in 2008 with the election of President Barack Obama significantly extended and intensified the war between the parties. The Republicans' smashing victory in the 2010 midterm elections, after two elections in 2006 and 2008 that were "waves" in favor of Democrats, produced yet another jump in the level of partisan polarization in the House, setting the stage for the debt ceiling fiasco that has come to exemplify the current dysfunctional politics.

There is no doubt that greater ideological agreement among members in both parties was a prerequisite to an increase in partisanship in Congress. Congressional scholars call it "conditional party government."[22] Like-minded party members representing more homogeneous constituencies are willing to delegate authority to their leaders to advance their collective electoral interests, putting a premium on strategic partisan team play. Building and maintaining each party's reputation dictate against splitting the difference in policy terms. It's better to have an issue than a bill, to shape the party's brand name and highlight party differences.[23] The extent of change toward tribalism is clear when party line voting spills over to issues with no discernable ideological content and where liberal and conservative positions are impossible to identify.[24]

Asymmetric Polarization: Not Your Mother's Republican Party
It is traditional that those in the American media intent on showing their lack of bias frequently report to their viewers and readers that both sides are equally guilty of partisan misbehavior. Journalistic traditions notwithstanding, reality is very different. The

center of gravity within the Republican Party has shifted sharply to the right. Its legendary moderate legislators in the House and Senate are virtually extinct. To be sure, a sizable number of the Republicans in Congress are center-right or right-center, rather than right-right. But the insurgent right wing regularly drowns them out. The post-McGovern Democratic Party, while losing the bulk of its conservative Dixiecrat contingent, has retained a more diverse constituency base, and since the Clinton presidency, has hewed to the center-left, with an emphasis on the center, on issues ranging from welfare reform to health policy.

Anyone who has reviewed the voluminous literature on the intellectual and organizational developments within the conservative movement and Republican Party since the 1970s will find that an unremarkable assertion.[25] The conservative critique of the Great Society social welfare programs and of the regulatory state, the mobilization of the Christian right, and the development of supply-side economics set the policy plate of the modern Republican Party. Over the course of the last three decades, the GOP has become the reflexive champion of lower taxes, reductions in the size and scope of the federal government, deregulation, and the public promotion of a religious and cultural conservatism. The striking changes in the nature of the Republican Party over the past fifty years are especially well documented in the book by political historian Geoffrey Kabaservice, *Rule and Ruin: The Downfall of Moderation and the Destruction of the Republican Party, From Eisenhower to the Tea Party*. He notes, "movement conservatism finally succeeded in silencing, co-opting, repelling, or expelling nearly every competing strain of Republicanism from the party, to the extent that the terms 'liberal Republican' or 'moderate Republican' have practically become oxymorons."[26]

Republican presidents Eisenhower and Nixon and congressional leaders such as Senators Everett Dirksen, Hugh Scott, Howard Baker, and Bob Dole, and Representatives Gerald Ford, John Rhodes, and Bob Michel, pragmatic institutional figures who found ways to work within the system and focused on solving problems, are unimaginable in the present context. President Reagan ushered in the new Republican Party but governed pragmatically. The steps he took in office, as well as those the two Bush presidents took, were so far outside the policy and procedural bounds of the contemporary GOP that none of them could likely win a Republican presidential nomination today without disavowing their own actions. Reagan was a serial violator of what we could call "Axiom One" for today's GOP, the no-tax-increase pledge: he followed his tax cuts of 1981 with tax increases in nearly every subsequent year of his presidency.[27] George H. W. Bush agreed to a 1990 deficit-reduction package that included tax increases and budget process reforms, turning back significant congressional Republican opposition (led by Newt Gingrich) along the way. And in more recent years, conservatives turned sharply against George W. Bush's advocacy of broad immigration reform (a violation of "Axiom Two"), expansion of government in health care and education (Oops! There goes "Axiom Three"), and steps to deal with the financial meltdown. That legacy, and Barack Obama's election and extraordinary measures to limit the damage from the financial crisis and deep recession, prompted the formation of a right-wing populist Tea Party movement, which the Republican establishment subsequently embraced.

Chuck Hagel, the former Republican Senator from Nebraska, echoed just these points in an August 2011 interview with the *Financial Times*. Hagel called his party "irresponsible" and said he was "disgusted" by the antics of the Republicans over the debt ceiling:

> The irresponsible actions of my party, the Republican Party over this were astounding. I'd never seen anything like this in my lifetime. . . . I was very disappointed. I was very disgusted in how this played out in Washington, this debt ceiling debate. It was an astounding lack of responsible leadership by many in the Republican Party, and I say that as a Republican. . . . I think the Republican Party is captive to political movements that are very ideological, that are very narrow. I've never seen so much intolerance as I see today in American politics.[28]

A veteran Republican congressional staffer, Mike Lofgren, wrote a long and anguished essay/diatribe in 2011 about why he ended his career on the Hill after nearly thirty years. His essay was filled with observations and broadsides like the following:

> It should have been evident to clear-eyed observers that the Republican Party is becoming less and less like a traditional political party in a representative democracy and becoming more like an apocalyptic cult, or one of the intensely ideological authoritarian parties of 20th century Europe.

He added,

> The only thing that can keep the Senate functioning is collegiality and good faith. During periods of political consensus, for instance, the World War II and early post-war eras, the Senate was a "high functioning" institution: filibusters were rare and the body was legislatively productive. Now, one can no more picture the current Senate producing

the original Medicare Act than the old Supreme Soviet having legislated the Bill of Rights.

Far from being a rarity, virtually every bill, every nominee for Senate confirmation and every routine procedural motion is now subject to a Republican filibuster. Under the circumstances, it is no wonder that Washington is gridlocked: legislating has now become war minus the shooting, something one could have observed 80 years ago in the Reichstag of the Weimar Republic. As Hannah Arendt observed, a disciplined minority of totalitarians can use the instruments of democratic government to undermine democracy itself.

And then this observation:

A couple of years ago, a Republican committee staff director told me candidly (and proudly) what the method was to all this obstruction and disruption. Should Republicans succeed in obstructing the Senate from doing its job, it would further lower Congress's generic favorability rating among the American people. By sabotaging the reputation of an institution of government, the party that is programmatically against government would come out the relative winner.[29]

Lofgren's frustration may make him more prone to hyperbole than other old-school Republicans—but his observations hit home with many of them, as they do with us.

The GOP's nearly unanimous pledge, in writing, not to increase taxes under any circumstance is perhaps the best indicator and most consequential component of its ideological thrust. Grover Norquist, president of Americans for Tax Reform and the man who fashioned the "Taxpayer Protection Pledge" to which Republicans pay fealty, has become a legendary power broker in the party. At the same time, its rank-and-file voters endorse the broader strategy the party elites have adopted, eschewing compromise to solve problems and insisting on sticking to principle even if it leads to gridlock.[30]

The Democrats under the presidencies of Clinton and Obama, by contrast, have become the more status-quo oriented, centrist protectors of government, willing to revamp programs and trim retirement and health benefits in order to maintain the government's central commitments in the face of fiscal pressures and global economic challenges.[31] And rank-and-file Democrats (along with self-identified Independents) favor compromise to solve problems over deadlock.[32]

The contrast plays out in a number of striking ways. One simple indicator is this: More than 70 percent of Republicans in the electorate identify themselves as conservative or very conservative, while only 40 percent of rank-and-file Democrats call themselves liberal or very liberal.[33] This difference at the level of mass politics is reflected in the ideological composition of the two parties in government. George W. Bush pushed through his signature tax cuts and Iraq war authorization with substantial Democratic support, while unwavering Republican opposition nearly torpedoed Barack Obama's health-care and financial reform legislation. When Democrats are in the majority, their greater ideological diversity combined with the unified opposition of Republicans induces the majority party to negotiate within its ranks, producing policies on health reform and climate change that not long ago would have attracted the support of at least a dozen Senate Republicans and thirty to forty House Republicans. Now? Zero in either chamber.

The phenomenon is even clearer when we look at roll call voting averages for parties on the same liberal-conservative

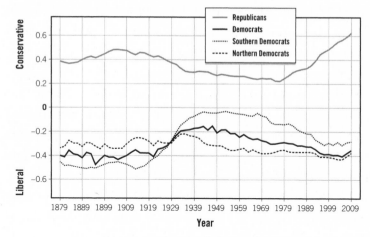

Figure 2-2 Liberal-Conservative Voting Averages in the House of Representatives 1879–2010.

dimension over time. Since the late 1970s, Republicans have moved much more sharply in a conservative direction than did Democrats in a liberal direction. And the change that occurred among Democrats was mostly within their Southern contingent—the demise of Dixiecrat conservatives and the election of minorities. Democratic representatives outside the South barely moved at all. (See Figure 2-2 for voting averages.[34]) The 2010 election dramatically increased the conservative tilt of the House Republicans. Nearly 80 percent of the freshmen Republicans in the 112th Congress would have been in the right wing of the party in the 111th Congress.[35]

Another indicator of the rightward shift of Republicans in Congress is the size of the House GOP's right-wing caucus, the Republican Study Committee, or RSC. Paul Weyrich and other conservative activists created the committee in 1973 as an informal group to pull the center-right party much further to the right; it had only 10 to 20 percent of Republican representatives as members as recently as the 1980s, a small fringe group. In the 112th Congress, the RSC had 166 members, or nearly seven-tenths of the caucus.

Relative ideological shifts between the two parties account for much, but not all of the asymmetric polarization. Part of their divergence stems from factors beyond ideology. As we discussed at the beginning of this chapter, the most important of these are side effects of the long and ultimately successful guerilla war that Newt Gingrich fashioned and led to end the hegemonic Democratic control of the House and national policy making. Other important factors are the rise of the new media and the culture of which it became an essential part, as well as the changing role of money and politics.

New Media and New Culture

As population shifts occurred and helped to trigger partisan and ideological movements, communications in the U.S. and the world were revolutionized, with dramatic implications for political discourse.[36] The media world in which we grew up in the 1950s was dominated by three television networks, which captured more than 70 percent of Americans as a regular viewing audience. A healthy majority relied on their news divisions, and especially the nightly news shows, as their primary source of information. Without remote controls, most Americans were passive consumers of that news. Second in line were newspapers. Most metropolitan areas had at least two and often more. While the editorial pages of the newspapers often had distinct party leanings, the news pages usually bent over backward to report news objectively, avoiding rumor or hearsay and relying on facts (with the exception of celebrity gossip columns in the tabloids).

Contrast that with the current situation. With the remarkable telecommunications revolution, there has been a veritable explosion of media. Adam Thierer of the Progress and Freedom Foundation pointed out in 2010 that there were almost 600 cable television channels, over 2,200 broadcast television stations, more than 13,000 over-the-air radio stations, over 20,000 magazines, and over 276,000 books published annually. As of December 2010, there were 255 million websites, and over 110 million domain names ending in .com, .net, and .org, and there were over 266 million Internet users in North America alone.[37]

Thierer also observed in early 2010:

> There are an estimated 26 million blogs on the Internet. YouTube reports that 20 hours of video are uploaded to the site every minute, and 1 billion videos are served up daily by YouTube, or 12.2 billion videos viewed per month. For video hosting site Hulu, as of Nov. 2009, 924 million videos were viewed per month in the U.S. Developers have created over 140,000 Apps for the Apple iPhone and iPod and iPad and made them available in the Apple App Store. Customers in 77 countries can choose apps in 20 categories, and users have downloaded over three billion apps since its [the iPhone's] inception in July 2008.[38]

The plethora of channels, websites, and other information options has fragmented audiences and radically changed media business models. The fragmentation also applies to attention spans. In 1950, the average weekly usage of a TV set was just over thirty hours, and the time per channel was twelve hours. By 2005, weekly TV set usage was up to nearly sixty hours, but time per channel was down to three hours. In the old days, the network news shows viewed themselves (and viewers deemed them so) as a public trust, were not required to be separate cost centers for their networks, and provided, along with newspapers and newsreels, a common set of facts and core of information that were widely shared.

Now, network news divisions have cut back dramatically on their news personnel and range of coverage as their share of viewers has declined to a tiny fraction of past numbers, and they rank far down as people's primary sources of information. The nightly news shows do provide a kind of headline service for viewers, but with more soft news about entertainment, lifestyle, and sports and with fewer in-depth pieces or extended interviews with sources. Local broadcast stations have found significant success with local news, but not of the political variety. Coverage of local elections or local politicians has declined dramatically.[39]

Cable news networks now compete with broadcast networks for news viewership. While their number of viewers remain less than the broadcast news channels, their business models enable them to be potentially more profitable. In 2010, Fox News returned a net profit of $700 million, more than the profits of the three network news divisions combined,[40] and one-fifth of Newscorp's total profits, despite the fact that Fox nightly news shows get around two million viewers, compared to the twenty million combined for the three network nightly newscasts. At the same time, broadcast news divisions are struggling and go through regular layoffs and cutbacks in domestic and international bureaus and of news personnel.

The Fox business model is based on securing and maintaining a loyal audience of conservatives eager to hear the same message presented in different ways by different hosts over and over again. MSNBC has adopted the Fox model on the left, in a milder form (especially in the daytime). CNN has tried multiple business models, but has settled on having regular showdowns pitting either a bedrock liberal against a bedrock conservative or a reliable spinner for Democrats against a Republican counterpart. For viewers, there is reinforcement that the only dialogue in the country is between polarized left and right, and that the alternative is cynical public relations with no convictions at all. The new business models and audiences are challenging the old notion that Americans can share a common set of facts and then debate options.

Pew Research Center studies have found that the audiences for Fox, CNN, and MSNBC are sharply different when it comes to partisan identity and ideology.[41] Another survey also noted differences between Fox viewers and the general public on attitudes and facts: "When compared against the general population, Fox News viewers are significantly less likely to believe that [President] Obama was born in the US, and that one of the most important problems facing the US is leadership. . . . Fox viewers are significantly less optimistic about the country's direction."[42] There is little doubt that Fox News is at least partly responsible for the asymmetric polarization that is now such a prominent feature of U.S. politics.

Newspapers, of course, are struggling even more than television networks. For years, polls showing declining readership among young generations forebode declining circulation. Because of waning ad revenues, especially from the bread-and-butter classified ads now supplanted by Craigslist and other online services like it, many newspapers have folded or merged with others for survival, creating more one-newspaper towns. Even more than networks, newspapers have reduced reporting corps and folded bureaus. One result has been the sharply reduced oversight of political figures and policy makers, and thus fewer checks and balances on their behavior.

America has gone back to the future with the new and prominent role of partisan media, just as in much of the nineteenth century but with far more reach, resonance, and scope than at any earlier period. The Fox News model—combative, partisan, sharp-edged—is the most successful business model by far in television news.

With the increased competition for eyeballs and readers, all media have become more focused on sensationalism and extremism, on infotainment over information, and, in the process, the culture has coarsened. No lie is too extreme to be published, aired, and repeated, with little or no repercussion for its perpetrator. The audiences that hear them repeatedly believe the lies, Obama's birthplace a prime example. A late-September 2011 Winthrop University survey of South Carolina Republicans found that 36 percent of those polled believed that the president was probably or definitely born outside the United States, a drop of only 5 percent from 41 percent in April, before the official release of his long-form birth certificate.[43] Barraged with media reports, including blogs and viral e-mails, and already convinced through years of messaging, these voters are inured to factual information. A world in which substantial numbers of Americans believe that the duly elected president of the United States is not legitimate is a world in which political compromise becomes substantially more difficult.

In a fragmented television and radio world of intense competition for eyeballs and eardrums sensationalism trumps sensible centrism. The lawmakers who get attention and airtime are the extreme and outrageous ones. For lawmakers, then, the new role models are people like Joe Wilson, Michele Bachmann, and Alan Grayson, the first two still in Congress. Outrageous comments result in celebrity status, huge fund-raising advantages, and more media exposure. Mild behavior or political centrism gets no such reward.

In addition to lawmakers, the bombastic and blustering figures in the political culture—the Ann Coulters, Michael Moores, and Erick Ericksons—are rewarded with huge book sales and cable jobs. Coulter's book titles range from *Godless* to *Slander* to *Guilty* to *Demonic* to *Treason*, all about liberals in America. The language is not conducive to debate and deliberation, but is now guaranteed to bring spots on the best-seller lists and huge lecture fees. Periodically, Coulter will say something so offensive and outrageous, or so wrong, that cable networks pledge to stop putting her on the air. That moratorium lasts, on average, for a few months, until the ratings drive in the new age overcomes the shame of showcasing a grenade-throwing extremist.

Beyond the bombast driven by the new media models, there are other sources of inflammatory rhetoric and misinformation, from tweets to blogs to viral e-mails. A good and persistent example of the latter is an e-mail that keeps circulating and being forwarded in bulk despite major efforts to debunk it. It reads in part:

> No one has been able to explain to me why young men and women serve in the U.S. Military for 20 years, risking their lives protecting freedom, and only get 50% of their pay. While politicians hold their political positions in the safe confines of the capital, protected by these same men and women, and receive full pay retirement after serving one term.
>
> Monday on Fox news they learned that the staffers of Congress family members are exempt from having to pay back student loans. . . .

For too long we have been too complacent about the workings of Congress. Many citizens had no idea that members of Congress could retire with the same pay after only one term, that they specifically exempted themselves from many of the laws they have passed (such as being exempt from any fear of prosecution for sexual harassment) while ordinary citizens must live under those laws. The latest is to exempt themselves from the Healthcare Reform . . . in all of its forms.[44]

In reality, all the "facts" in the e-mail are wrong. Here's a Congressional Research Service report on pensions:

Congressional pensions, like those of other federal employees, are financed through a combination of employee and employer contributions. . . . Members of Congress are eligible for a pension at age 62 if they have completed at least five years of service. Members are eligible for a pension at age 50 if they have completed 20 years of service, or at any age after completing 25 years of service. The amount of the pension depends on years of service and the average of the highest three years of salary. By law, the starting amount of a Member's retirement annuity may not exceed 80% of his or her final salary.

As of October 1, 2006, 413 retired Members of Congress were receiving federal pensions based fully or in part on their congressional service. Of this number, 290 had retired under [the Civil Service Retirement System] and were receiving an average annual pension of $60,972. A total of 123 Members had retired with service under both CSRS and [the Federal Employees Retirement System] or with service under FERS only. Their average annual pension was $35,952 in 2006.[45]

On the Fox News assertion about student loans, this from factcheck.org (responding to dozens of inquiries):

> Are members of Congress exempt from repaying student loans?
>
> Are members' families exempt from having to pay back student loans?
>
> Are children of members of Congress exempted from repaying their student loans?
>
> Do congressional staffers have to pay back their student loans?
>
> The answers are: no, no, no and yes—although some full-time congressional staffers participate in a student loan repayment program that helps pay back a portion of student loans. No more than $60,000 in the House and $40,000 in the Senate can be forgiven and only if the employee stays on the job for several years.[46]

The assertion that members of Congress are exempt from the provisions of the Affordable Care Act is also false. Members of Congress are subject under the health-care reform law to the same mandate as others to purchase insurance, and their plans must have the same minimum standards of benefits that other insurance plans will have to meet. Members of Congress currently have no gold-plated free plan, but the same insurance options that most other federal employees have, and they do not get it free. They have a generous subsidy for their premiums, but no more generous (and, compared to many businesses or professions, less generous) than standard employer-provided subsidies throughout the country.[47]

This e-mail is a new political version of an urban legend, but with serious consequences. Former Senator Robert Bennett

(R-Utah) has reported that a Tea Party activist who challenged Bennett's renomination to the Senate (he was blocked from even running for reelection as a Republican in 2010) said he was motivated to run by that e-mail. The exaggerated views of politicians reinforced here enhance the anti-politician populism that fueled the Tea Party movement. In the new age and the new culture, the negative and false charges are made rapidly and are hard to counter or erase. They also make rational discourse in campaigns and in Congress more difficult and vastly more expensive.

Viral e-mails and word-of-mouth campaigns are expanding sharply, mostly aimed at false facts about political adversaries. As the *Washington Post*'s Paul Farhi notes in an article titled, "The e-mail rumor mill is run by conservatives," they are overwhelmingly coming from the right and are aimed at President Obama and other liberals—and they are powerful:

> Grass-roots whisper campaigns such as these predate the invention of the "send" button, of course. No one needed a Facebook page or an e-mail account to spread the word about Thomas Jefferson's secret love child or Grover Cleveland's out-of-wedlock offspring (both won elections despite the stories, which in Jefferson's case were very likely true).
>
> But it has become a truism that in their modern, Internet-driven form, these persistent narratives spread far faster and run deeper than ever. And they share an unexpected trait: Most of the time, Democrats (or liberals) are the ones under attack. Yes, George W. Bush had some whoppers told about him—such as his alleged scoffing that the French "don't have a word for 'entrepreneur' "—but when it comes to generating and sustaining specious and shocking stories, there's no contest. The majority of the junk comes from the right, aimed at the left.

We're not talking here about verifiably inaccurate statements from the mouths of politicians and party leaders. There's plenty of that from all sides. And almost all of those statements are out in the open, where they get called out relatively quickly by the opposition or the mainstream media.

Instead, it's the sub rosa campaigns of vilification, the can-you-believe-this beauts that land periodically in your inbox from a trusted friend or relative amid the noise of every political season.

This sort of buzz occurs out of earshot of the news media. It gains rapid and broad circulation by being passed from hand to hand, from friend to relative to co-worker. Its power and credibility come from its source. . . .

Of the 79 chain e-mails about national politics deemed false by PolitiFact since 2007, only four were aimed at Republicans. Almost all of the rest concern Obama or other Democrats. The claims range from daffy (the White House renaming Christmas trees as "holiday trees") to serious (the health-care law granting all illegal immigrants free care).[48]

The impact of all this is to reinforce tribal divisions, while enhancing a climate where facts are no longer driving debate and deliberation, nor are they shared by the larger public.

Money in Politics

Author Robert Kaiser struck a chord when he titled his recent book *So Damn Much Money*.[49] American elections are awash in money, politicians devote an inordinate amount of their time dialing for dollars, and campaign fund-raising is now considered a normal part of the lobbying process.

Kaiser's book was mostly about lobbying. In a city where much of the business is about divvying up over $3 trillion in federal spending and carving out tax breaks from over $2 trillion in revenues, the money spent on influencing those decisions has mushroomed, and the money that lobbyists and their associates make has become almost mind-boggling. The corruption that Kaiser describes—direct and indirect, from literal or near bribes and the trading of favors to the insidious corruption of the revolving door, where lawmakers and other public officials leave office and become highly paid lobbyists asking for favors from their former colleagues and using their expertise to influence the passage and implementation of laws and regulations—has moved from a chronic problem to an acute one. It was dampened a bit after the uproar of the Jack Abramoff–Tom DeLay era that ended with Abramoff's conviction and DeLay's departure from Congress in 2006, or perhaps more accurately, in 2010 with the conviction of Kevin Ring, one of Abramoff's associates, over a series of bribes and lavish perks provided to lawmakers and staff in return for legislative benefits. But the money in Washington and the problems of the revolving door have barely abated and, with the new era of campaign finance since the Supreme Court's *Citizens United* decision, have in many ways become shockingly worse.

In 2011, Jack Abramoff himself came out of exile as a repentant sinner and talked openly about the corrupt system in Washington, vividly describing the depth of rot. On November 6, 2011, Abramoff appeared on *60 Minutes* and described how he had corrupted congressional staffers:

> When we would become friendly with an office and they were important to us, and the chief of staff was a competent person, I would say or my staff would say to him or her at some point, "You know, when you're done working on the

Hill, we'd very much like you to consider coming to work for us." Now the moment I said that to them or any of our staff said that to 'em, that was it. *We owned them. And what does that mean? Every request from our office, every request of our clients, everything that we want, they're gonna do. And not only that, they're gonna think of things we can't think of to do.*[50]

While Abramoff was caught and served prison time, the fundamentals of the system he described have not changed. If other lobbyists do not operate with his flamboyance, the system awash in money still operates as it did in 2006. One vivid example is "Newt, Inc.," the name observers of Newt Gingrich coined after he left Congress. The industrious Gingrich created a web of for-profit and not-for-profit groups that garnered nearly $150 million in fees from a wide array of businesses and trade associations. Newt's influence-for-hire operation included the now well-publicized $1.6 million to $1.8 million from Freddie Mac to legitimize its efforts with House Republicans, and over $30 million from health-care-related organizations. Gingrich said he did no lobbying, but of course, it's hard to figure out what his clients were buying other than access to policy makers.

To be sure, money has long played a problematic role in American democracy. Reconciling the tension between economic inequality and political equality, while preserving the constitutional guarantee of free speech, is no easy task. A healthy democracy with open and competitive elections requires ample resources for candidates to be heard and voters to garner the information they need to make considered decisions. This country has regulated campaign finance for over a century, though often with weak and porous statutes and grossly inadequate means of enforcement.[51] A major increase in recent decades in the demand for and supply of money in politics directly exacerbates dysfunctional politics by threatening the independence and integrity of policy makers and by reinforcing partisan polarization.

The first flows from the inadequate measures to limit the source and size of contributions to candidates and parties. Prohibitions on corporate contributions in federal elections were enacted early in the twentieth century; these were extended to direct spending as well as contributions from corporations and unions in the 1940s. Violations of these laws by the Committee to Reelect the President in the 1972 election led to the passage of a more ambitious regulatory regime that added contribution limits, public funding of presidential campaigns, and more effective public disclosure.

By the 1990s, parties found ways of raising so-called soft money—unlimited contributions from corporations, unions, and individuals ostensibly used for purposes other than influencing federal elections. The availability of these unrestricted sources of campaign funds created increased opportunities for inappropriate pressure and conflicts of interest if not outright extortion or bribery between public officials and private interests.

Stories of politicians using elaborate inducements to raise huge sums of soft money from big donors (including sleepovers in the Lincoln Bedroom and—literally—menus of intimate access to key committee chairs in Congress or top party leaders based on levels of soft money contributions) led to a drive for major reform. It was intensified by the growing impact of "independent" outside and party ads, financed by soft money from individuals, corporations, and unions, using a loophole in the regulations that allowed unlimited funds for so-called "issue ads." The ads did not say explicitly "elect" or "defeat" a candidate, but in every other respect were aimed at voters in a district or state to influence the election outcomes.

The Bipartisan Campaign Reform Act (known widely as the McCain-Feingold Act), passed in 2002, was designed to prohibit party soft money and to bring electioneering communications (those campaign ads parading as issue ads) under the contribution and disclosure restrictions of the law. The Supreme Court upheld it in 2003, in *McConnell v. Federal Election Commission*.

That law worked as intended, until it was overwhelmed by a series of Supreme Court decisions, which, in combination with a lax Federal Election Commission and increasingly brazen entrepreneurs pushing the boundaries of the law beyond recognition, have created the political equivalent of a new Wild West. *Citizens United v. Federal Election Commission*, decided by a 5–4 majority in 2010, was the centerpiece of the Court's recent deregulatory juggernaut to overturn decades of law and precedent. In a breathtaking breach of judicial norms dealing with cases and controversies and legal precedents, the Court ruled that corporations and unions were free to make unlimited independent expenditures in elections for public office. Step back for a moment and look at the trajectory of this case.[52] The plaintiff, Citizens United (a conservative group), narrowly challenged a provision of the 2002 Bipartisan Campaign Reform Act to enable in this situation unlimited corporate advertising funding for a "documentary" film called *Hillary: The Movie*. The film was unabashedly designed to derail Hillary Rodham Clinton's campaign for president. Citizens United wanted only an "as applied" exception for their documentary, which they believed did not meet the standard of "electioneering communications" in the law. They explicitly did not raise the larger question of overturning the ban on corporate spending in federal campaigns.

The Justices heard the case on that basis, but Chief Justice John Roberts, with support from his allies on the Court, decided unilaterally to raise the broader issue of whether a prohibition on corporations' independent expenditures was constitutional, and he demanded a rehearing. That 5–4 ruling overturned decades of established doctrine, throwing the world of campaign finance into turmoil and demonstrating a troubling new approach to governance by the Supreme Court. The willingness to do something dramatic and highly controversial on a 5–4 vote, underscoring the pattern set in 2000 by the 5–4 highly charged decision that decided the outcome of the presidential election, *Bush v. Gore*, was accompanied by what we believe was a reckless approach to jurisprudence.

The sweep and scope of the decision was especially disturbing, given what Chief Justice nominee Roberts had vowed at his confirmation hearings in front of the Senate Judiciary Committee in September 2005. In his opening statement, he said:

> Judges and justices are servants of the law, not the other way around. They make sure everybody plays by the rules. But it is a limited role. Nobody ever went to a ball game to see the umpire. Judges have to have the humility to recognize that they operate within a system of precedents, shaped by other judges equally striving to live up to the judicial oath. . . . I will remember that it is my job to call balls and strikes and not to pitch or bat.
>
> I do think that it is a jolt to the legal system when you overrule a precedent. . . . It is not enough that you may think the prior decision was wrongly decided. . . . The role of the judge is limited; the judge is to decide the cases before them; they're not to legislate; they're not to execute the laws.

Now add the comments Roberts made a year later at the Georgetown University Law Center commencement: "The broader the agreement among the justices, the more likely it is that the decision is on the narrowest possible ground." He added: "If it is not necessary to decide more to dispose of a case, in my view it is necessary not to decide more."[53]

Judges and Congresses in the past had carefully considered the cases overturned and the laws struck down in *Citizens United*, including in the *McConnell* decision barely six years earlier. Only one thing had changed—the political and ideological complexion of the Supreme Court brought on in particular by the retirement of Sandra Day O'Connor. Had O'Connor not retired, *Citizens United* either would not have been broadened or would have been decided 5–4 the other way.

Justice Anthony Kennedy, who drew on reasoning that struck pragmatic observers of money and politics as bizarre, authored the *Citizens United* decision. He equated money with speech and equated corporations, which have the one goal of making money, with individual citizens, who have many goals and motives in their lives, including making a better society, protecting their children and grandchildren and future generations, and so on. And, as legal scholar Richard Hasen recently noted, Kennedy added gratuitously in the decision his flat statement: "We now conclude that independent expenditures, including those made by corporations, do not give rise to corruption or the appearance of corruption."[54] That statement, belied by the everyday experience of politicians and lobbyists throughout Washington, has opened the floodgates to even more money in politics, and more corruption.

It has also resulted in a substantial infection of judicial elections—something Kennedy, in an earlier opinion (*Caperton v. A.T. Massey Coal*) had decried, saying (ironically, given his reasoning in *Citizens United*) that independent expenditures *could* corrupt judges and courts. A new report by the Brennan Center at New York University looking at judicial elections in 2009–2010 noted: "Nearly 40% of all funds spent on state high court races came from just 10 groups, including national special interest groups and political parties; nearly 1/3 of all funds spent on state high court elections came from non-candidate groups ($11.5 million out of $38 million in 2009-10); and, though outside groups paid for only 40% of total ads, they were responsible for 3 in 4 attack ads."[55]

Sure enough, in the wake of *Citizens United*, political operatives stepped in with creative ways to push the envelope and use huge sums of money both to influence campaigns and to shape legislative outcomes, and to brazenly evade the disclosure requirements for donors that were upheld by the Supreme Court. In one particularly egregious example, former Bush adviser Karl Rove and former Republican National Committee chair Ed Gillespie created two political organizations called American Crossroads. The first, under Section 527 of the Internal Revenue Code, was required to disclose its donors. But the ever-creative Rove also launched a *second* group, American Crossroads GPS, this one a 501(c)4 under the tax code designed for nonprofit social welfare advocacy organizations. The important thing about these groups is that they don't have to disclose donors. The second group raised $5.1 million in June 2010 alone, with a goal of reaching $50 million for that election, and according to media accounts, succeeded in its fund-raising because it tapped into sources that did not want to be identified. The "concept paper" describing for potential donors the reasons to support American Crossroads GPS said the group will conduct "in-depth research on congressional expense account abuses," to blame Democrats for "failed border controls" and to frame the BP oil spill as "Obama's Katrina."[56]

It is impossible to imagine that American Crossroads GPS has any purpose other than electing Republican candidates while keeping the fat-cat donor names hidden from public view. As *Politico* reporter Ken Vogel noted, Rove created the spinoff group so donors wouldn't have to be publicly associated with him.[57]

Rove is not the only political operative seizing on this loophole in IRS regulations to do aggressive partisan campaigning. In February 2010, former Senator Norm Coleman formed a 501(c)4 "action tank" called the American Action Network, which spent a large sum of money in 2010 on attack ads hitting Governor Charlie Crist, who ran as an Independent in the Florida Senate race, and Senator Patty Murray (D-Wash.) in her campaign. Its sister 501(c)3, called American Action Forum, is its "think tank." Not surprisingly, unions and other liberal and Democratic groups have followed suit, creating a money arms race to attract anonymous large donors.

Given that both parties are exploiting the nonprofit loophole, it would be easy to blame them both equally, and media reinforce that tendency. In a January 27, 2012, CNN piece, anchor Erin Burnett called it "Democratic and Republican bipartisan loophole action." Her guest, *Politico* reporter David Levinthal added, "Well, of course, the Democrats want to blame the Republicans and the Republicans want to blame the Democrats, but you're right. This is not exclusive to any one party and is this going to change? Well, Congress tried to change it back in 2010. They tried to pass a piece of legislation called the DISCLOSE Act. Well it went nowhere."

In fact, the blame for evasion of disclosure laws is heavily tilted to the Republican side. The leaders in the effort to evade disclosure laws have been Republicans, and the Democrats' united effort to create a robust disclosure regime after *Citizens United* was thwarted on a filibuster in the Senate in 2010 when all fifty-nine Democrats voted for the DISCLOSE Act, but could not get a single Senate Republican, including reformers like John McCain and Olympia Snowe, to provide the necessary sixtieth vote to overcome the filibuster.

Along with the misuse of nonprofit status to evade disclosure, the *Citizens United* decision, combined with the D.C. Circuit Court of Appeals decision in *SpeechNow v. Federal Election Commission*, resulted in a new vehicle to erase any campaign contribution limits.[58] The *SpeechNow* decision said that so-called independent-expenditure committees, which can attack or defend candidates directly, could receive contributions in unlimited amounts, that is, via soft money. This meant the creation of what have been called "super PACs" (now made famous by TV host Stephen Colbert, who created his own), which have exploded on the scene since 2010. Super PACs are in theory not allowed to coordinate with candidates and are required to disclose contributors. But it is a measure of how farcical the law's remaining constraints are that 2012 presidential candidates' closest advisers are forming super PACs on their behalf as an obvious way to evade campaign contribution limits. Even sitting members of Congress are trying to blow the remaining limits on soft money out of the water by creating their own super PACs.[59]

A group of candidate Mitt Romney's former aides, friends, and business associates formed a super PAC called "Restore Our Future," ostensibly independent of Romney's campaign. But the founders included his former campaign general counsel, former political director, and former media team leader. Beyond the super PAC itself, the Romney effort shows that the temptation for chicanery is great. In mid-2011, a mystery donor had a Massachusetts tax lawyer form a sham corporation with the sole purpose of donating $1 million to Restore Our Future; as soon as the contribution was made, the corporation disbanded.[60] Only after a major public uproar did the donor identify himself: Edward Conard, the former managing director of the Romney-founded Bain Capital. Despite the obvious attempt to evade disclosure requirements, the Romney super PAC took the money and declared the controversy over once Conard's name became public.[61]

Romney, of course, was not alone among presidential candidates in making sure that super PACs arose so the candidates could avoid presidential campaign contribution limits. Candidate Rick Perry's close friend and former staffer from his governor's office, Mike Toomey, created a Perry super PAC, "Make Us Great Again." Toomey earlier had settled civil litigation for his efforts to get the Texas Association of Business to funnel $1.7 million in secret corporate contributions to Texas legislative candidates. He had also secretly financed an effort to get the Green Party on the ballot in Texas in 2010 to siphon votes from Perry's Democratic opponent in the gubernatorial campaign. Andrew Wheat, the research director of Texans for Public Justice, commented, "Rick Perry and Mike Toomey have been attached at the hip for 25 years. Any suggestion that these Siamese twins operate independently of one another is a legal fiction."[62]

Congressional leaders have not been far behind in the super PAC race. John Murray, a top adviser to House Majority Leader Eric Cantor, left Cantor's staff in October 2011 to form a super PAC, a 501(c)4, and a nonprofit educational entity known as a 501(c)3, all to help elect "pro-market candidates" (and not coincidentally use the unlimited super PAC and unlimited and anonymous 501(c)4 contributions to help advance Cantor). Congressional Democratic leaders have not formed their own super PACs, but House Minority Leader Nancy Pelosi has raised money for a super PAC called House Majority PAC, while Senate Majority Leader Harry Reid has raised money for Majority PAC, a counterpart advancing Democratic candidates for the Senate.

The out-of-control money system is showing itself in big and corrupting ways in Congress.[63] We have had conversations with several incumbents in the Senate up for election in 2012. They say the same thing: they can handle any of the several prospective opponents they might face, but all of them fear a stealth campaign landing behind their lines and spending $20 million on "independent" efforts designed to portray the incumbent as a miscreant and scoundrel who should be behind bars, not serving in the Senate. And, of course, the contributors to the campaign would be undisclosed.

Most politicians understand that constituents who like or approve of them don't really know much about them; voters don't spend a lot of time focusing on politics and politicians. So a vicious and unrelenting negative ad campaign can work. What do candidates do then? Beyond the money they raise directly for their campaigns against their opponents, they are working overtime to raise their own protective war chests, meaning they spend every spare moment not deliberating or debating policy, but on "call time," begging for money. Time spent this way means less time to spend with colleagues, and since the money raised in many cases will go directly into campaigns of vilification against other lawmakers, it is not exactly conducive to working together.

Many lobbyists in Washington will add another twist to the new post–*Citizens United* world. We have heard the same story over and over: a lobbyist meets with a lawmaker to advocate for a client, and before he gets back to the office, the lawmaker calls asking for money. The connections between policy actions or inactions and fund-raising are no longer indirect or subtle.

Then there is a third element. As one Senator said to us, "We have all had experiences like the following: A lobbyist or interest representative will be in my office. He or she will say, 'You know, Americans for a Better America really, really want this amendment passed. And they have more money than God. I don't know what they will do with their money if they don't get what they want. But they are capable of spending a fortune to make anybody who disappoints them regret it.'" No money has to be spent to get the desired outcome.

Writer Jane Mayer's October 10, 2011, article in *The New Yorker* recounted the chilling story of wealthy North Carolina businessman Art Pope who spent tens of millions of dollars to buy (with apparent success) a state legislature to his liking. Reinforcing the point about destructive polarization, Mayer shows that Pope's money paid for vicious ads that attacked the integrity of incumbent moderate Democrats and moderate Republicans—to eliminate the center, discourage others of a moderate mind-set from running, and create yet more polarization, this time at the state level. And one major result of his efforts was partisan gerrymandering in North Carolina in 2011 that has targeted three of the few remaining centrist "Blue Dog" Democrats in the House for extinction.[64]

This is just the beginning. Each week seems to bring yet another new initiative by candidates, parties, or private interests to set up parallel political organizations and escape all restrictions on money in politics. The independence, integrity, and legitimacy of government are the victims.

These developments in campaign finance work in multiple ways to reinforce the partisan polarization at the root of dysfunctional politics. Parties are at the center, not the periphery, of fundraising. They expect members of Congress to raise money for the team through their personal campaign committees and leadership PACs, so that resources can be redistributed from safe to competitive seats. Party leaders are prolific fund-raisers, as are aspiring leaders. They expect committee and subcommittee chairs to use their positions to raise campaign funds for the party. Becoming a committee chair can depend more on one's fund-raising prowess than one's legislative or policy skills or knowledge. Many of the super PACs and other independent groups are effectively extensions of the parties, part of the multilayered coalitions that constitute today's political parties.[65] These fund-raising and spending arrangements provide special opportunities for generous donors and spenders, many (like the infamous Koch brothers who have created a web of well-financed conservative groups with innocuous names to promote their ideological and business interests) with extreme ideological views and direct stakes in public policy decisions to shape the positions and agendas of the parties.

Many parts of this story are familiar to readers who have been watching Washington and American politics. Many stories, as we have said, are variations on age-old themes or amplifications of earlier trends. We constantly have to ask ourselves whether all this is truly any different from the past, or even different from what we remember through rosy gauze from previous decades. But our conclusion is firm: the combination of old trends, new technologies, new players, and a coarsened political culture has passed a critical point, leading to something far more troubling than we have ever seen.[66]

III **3** III

Beyond the Debt Ceiling Fiasco

I f the debt ceiling mess were the only example of a political system gone wild, it would be easy to say either that it was an anomaly or that the inherent messiness of a disputatious political process—one built around, as the late constitutional scholar Edward Corwin put it, "an invitation to struggle" among and across the branches—makes such showdowns inevitable.[1] But the current situation is different. If the politics of partisan confrontation, parliamentary-style maneuvering, and hostage taking has been building since the late 1970s, it has become far more the norm than the exception since Barack Obama's election. In 2009–2010, when the Democrats controlled the House and Senate as well as the White House, it was all about drawing sharp partisan lines in the dust, with no Republican votes available for any major legislative initiative, save the three Senate Republicans who voted early on for the economic stimulus in return for major concessions to each of them. Since then, the focus has been on Republican unwillingness to cooperate or work with the president except under duress or in an area, like that of free trade agreements with Colombia, Panama, and South Korea, that had long been GOP goals.

In the case of the third prong of the Eric Cantor strategy we outlined in Chapter 1—the continuing resolution standoff for fiscal 2012—Cantor demanded for the first time offsets from other social programs to pay for emergency disaster-relief spending after Hurricane Irene and other natural disasters. At a time when people across the Northeast were confronting mortal threats and devastating personal losses, Cantor and his allies piled on additional anxiety over whether the government was going to help them out or divert their disaster aid to other regions. At the same time, Republicans upped the hostage ante, since paying directly and immediately for disaster relief would mean cutting critical programs like food safety and health research, which had already been hit with budget cutbacks in the fiscal 2011 budget.

Even more troubling was a spat over the Federal Aviation Administration (FAA) in the summer of 2011. John Mica, the Republican chairman of the House Transportation and Infrastructure Committee, issued a set of nonnegotiable demands to senators during negotiations over a long-stalled reauthorization of the FAA.[2] For many months, lawmakers had regularly extended FAA authority temporarily while they negotiated their differences. Mica, though, insisted that he would no longer keep the agency operating in the absence of an agreement. He would kill any reauthorization unless Democrats in the Senate agreed to reverse a ruling permitting FAA employees to bargain in the same way as other federal employee unions and shut off subsidies to small airports, the latter having especially dire consequences for the key negotiating senators, Jay Rockefeller of West Virginia and Max Baucus of Montana.

There was a case to be made that the subsidies to small and sparsely used airports were an unnecessary use of taxpayer dollars. But Mica's efforts were not aimed at all such airports, only those in his rival counterparts' states. At the same time, Mica spurned efforts to compromise on airport subsidies, since they did not include the union bargaining part of his wish list.

When Senate Democrats wouldn't accede to his demands, Mica refused to continue authorizing the agency and let the House adjourn without action. Again, the consequences to American citizens were considerable. Major parts of the FAA were shut down for several weeks, putting thousands of workers on furlough and requiring airplane inspectors to work without pay and cover their own travel expenses out of pocket in order to keep airplanes safe and flying. Around 24,000 construction workers lost their jobs, with many thousands of other jobs directly and indirectly lost, causing untold suffering and halting work at the peak period for construction of airport facilities, runways, hangars, and other operations. The urgently needed new generation of computerized air-traffic control lost critical weeks of development, and the FAA could not collect airfare taxes for several weeks, costing the federal treasury some $300 million. The savings Mica insisted upon by ending the subsidies to the small airports was a small fraction of that amount.

Ultimately, Senate Democrats accepted a short-term provision giving Mica some of what he wanted, but that was reversed under intense public and media pressure after the House returned and Mica gave in. But for weeks, one individual's "my way or the highway" pique, framed in part as a fiscal conservative's demand to cut out wasteful subsidies to underutilized rural airports, caused economic havoc way out of proportion to the magnitude of the problem and leading to a major increase in the deficit, instead of a consensual approach to reducing the subsidies. A somewhat chastened Mica, hurt by the wave of criticism, said defensively that he had just been trying to end business as usual. But if ending business as usual in Washington means adding to the debt and causing economic and social disruption in order to force a tiny sum in savings, it is not a desirable route to take.

In the past, tough negotiators who played hardball had a basic respect for their opponents and some sensitivity to the consequences of their tactics. They did not try gleefully to embarrass their counterparts in the other body or the other party to score political points, or push so far that the collateral damage of their actions truly hurt large numbers of Americans. Add to that the cynical exploitation of the rules to demolish the regular order in Congress and to damage policy deliberation in the service of the permanent campaign. That problem starts with the abuse of Rule XXII, the filibuster rule.[3]

Holds and Filibusters

The Senate is a slow-moving institution at its core, one that bends over backward to accommodate its one hundred oversized egos. Where the House is built around collective action, with rules to expedite it, the Senate is built around individual actors, with much of its ability to act requiring unanimous consent. Respect for the individual is one thing, but in recent years, the Senate has increasingly seen individual senators hold their colleagues and the larger government hostage to their whims and will. More and more, senators have blocked bills and nominations by the informal practice of the "hold," basically an individual senator's notification to the leadership in writing that he or she will object to consideration of a bill or nomination.

Because the individualized Senate operates mostly via unanimous consent to schedule and expedite its business, this practice has a significant effect. (The larger and more disciplined House operates by majority vote.) If any one senator denies that unanimous consent, it requires the majority leader to jump through many hoops and take much precious time to slate a bill or move to confirm a nominee. In past decades, when a senator invoked a hold to deny unanimous consent, the common practice was to allow an absent senator to delay deliberation on the bill or nomination until he or she could be there for the debate or vote, or to allow an unprepared senator to have the time to muster his or her arguments to debate on the floor, meaning a delay of a week or two. Holds, however, have morphed into indefinite or permanent vetoes, often done secretly, with members of each party using nominations as hostages to extract concessions from the executive branch.

We have seen outrageous examples of individual pique holding up dozens or hundreds of nominations. For example, in May 2003, then Senator Larry Craig of Idaho, trying to bludgeon the Air Force into stationing four cargo planes in his state, anonymously blocked all Air Force promotions for months until investigative reporters unmasked his secret hold. In February 2010, Senator Richard Shelby of Alabama put a blanket hold on all White House nominations for executive positions (over seventy were pending at the time) in order to get two earmarks worth tens of billions of dollars fast-tracked for his state. Before eventual confirmation, President Obama's nomination for Commerce Secretary, California utility and energy executive John Bryson, was held up for months despite his sterling qualifications by a succession of Senate Republicans, leaving the Commerce Department leaderless at a critical time. These tactics were not unprecedented. Democratic Leader Harry Reid in 2004 openly held up a number of appointments (he exempted military and judicial nominees) in order to get his nominee to the Nuclear Regulatory Commission approved. But blanket holds have become much more frequent and disruptive in the last several years.

The hold is in effect a threat to filibuster a bill or nomination. And the filibuster, the infamous process that requires a super-majority to overcome an intense minority in the Senate, can have profound implications for the ability to govern and to make policy. Here, the minority party's sharply expanded use of the hold as a political tactic to delay and block action by the majority has transformed the Senate, especially over the past four years.

It is now ingrained as conventional wisdom that the filibuster and unlimited debate either are in the Constitution or have long been an integral part of the Senate. That assumption is wrong. The framers of the Constitution did not establish the basis for unlimited debate in the Senate, but senators introduced it in the first decade of the nineteenth century. The first Senates had the same provision as the House of Representatives, to allow a simple majority to stop debate and move to a vote, something called in parliamentary parlance "moving the previous question."[4]

In an unintended quirk that changed history, Vice President Aaron Burr, in his 1805 farewell address to the Senate, suggested that it clean up its rule book, eliminating duplicative and extraneous rules, among them the previous-question motion. The Senate had no intention of allowing unlimited debate, but from that point on, any senator could take to the floor and hold it as long as he or she could stay there. It was several decades before any senator took advantage of the quirk, and even after, the move to block action by debating nonstop was rare.[5] The lack of any rule or process to limit debate lasted until 1917, when a filibuster over efforts to rearm America in preparation for World War I by just five senators—an angry President Woodrow Wilson called them "a little band of willful men"—endangered American preparedness. That led to a backlash and a new rule allowing cloture—stopping the debate—if two-thirds of senators voting agreed. (The rule, XXII, stayed more or less intact until the 1970s, when the number required to stop the debate was reduced to sixty senators.)

Filibusters and their sister element, cloture motions to end debate and move to a vote, were extremely rare events after the advent of Rule XXII, but they carried with them an almost romantic notion of the power of individuals who feel intensely about an issue to grab the attention of the Senate and the country. Of course, the embodiment of that sentiment came in the 1939 movie *Mr. Smith Goes to Washington*, when Jimmy Stewart seized the Senate floor and spoke until hoarse and then until he collapsed, all in the name of ending the power of a corrupt political boss from his unnamed state.

"Mr. Smith" was thoroughly fictional, and in the real world, attempts at filibuster and formal responses to them—meaning actual cloture motions to shut off debate—remained relatively rare, even during the civil rights era of the 1950s and 1960s. The number of cloture motions did increase after that, mostly because a handful of individual conservative senators, especially Democrat James Allen of Alabama and Republican Jesse Helms of North Carolina, seeing the role of Southern conservatives as a bloc decline, began to use more creative ways to gain leverage. This included finding ways to extend debate after a filibuster was invoked by offering hundreds of amendments and insisting on a vote on each. Still, even with Allen remaining active until his death in 1978, the average number of cloture motions filed in a given month was less than two; it increased to around three a month in the 1980s, jumped a bit in the 1990s during the Clinton presidency, and then leveled off in the early Bush years. But starting in 2006, this number spiked dramatically and even more with the election of Barack Obama.[6] In the 110th Congress, 2007–2008, and in the 111th Congress, the number of cloture motions filed when the Senate was in session was on the order of two a week! (See Figure 3-1 for the number of motions from 1965 through 2010.)

The sharp jump in cloture motions came in response to the increasingly routine use of the filibuster. No longer is it just a tool of last resort, used only in rare cases when a minority with a strong belief on an issue of major importance attempts to bring the process to a screeching halt to focus public attention on its grievances. When Southern Democrats filibustered civil rights bills, they wanted to show their constituents and the broader American public why they were standing on the tracks to prevent the civil rights train from advancing and, in their view, destroying their way of life.

Now, since 2006, but especially since Obama's inauguration in 2009, the filibuster is more often a stealth weapon, which minority Republicans use not to highlight an important national issue but to delay and obstruct quietly on nearly all matters, including routine and widely supported ones. It is fair to say that this pervasive use of the filibuster has never before happened in the history of the Senate.[7]

There's no doubt that the increase in cloture motions is a two-way street, reflecting changes by both parties. The minority has moved to erect a filibuster bar for nearly everything. The majority has moved preemptively to cut off delays by invoking cloture at the start of the process, prior to any negotiations with the minority over the terms of debate, and to avoid politically charged amendments that might put some of their members in a

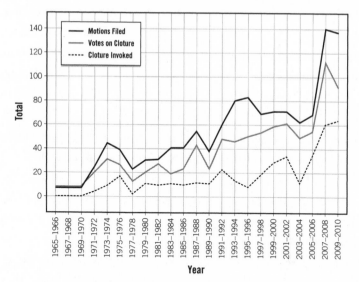

Figure 3-1 Cloture Motions in the Senate, 1965–2010.

difficult position back home by limiting the minority's ability to offer amendments.[8]

Invoking cloture means that sixty senators vote to stop debate and move to a resolution of the underlying bill or nomination (albeit after an additional sizable delay of at least thirty hours for additional debate). You might think that there would be a cloture motion only if a matter were so contentious that it deeply divided the Senate. But the increase in cloture motions in the past five years has been matched by an increase in their rate of success. Senators threatened filibusters or imposed holds on measures that were in fact not deeply contentious and controversial, but that easily passed the bar of sixty votes without any Mr. Smith–style filibustering on the floor. This is more evidence that senators have distorted a practice designed for rare use—to let a minority of any sort have its say in matters of great national significance—to serve other purposes. One purpose is rank obstruction, to use as much precious time as possible on the floor of the Senate to retard progress on business the majority wants to conduct, and to make everything look contentious and messy so that voters will react against the majority and against the policies the senators do manage to enact. These increased incentives for obstruction in the policy-making process are intimately tied to the intense competition for control of Congress and the White House.[9]

Consider three examples from the 111th Congress. The first is H.R. 3548, the Worker, Homeownership, and Business Assistance Act of 2009, pushed by the Obama administration and Senate Democrats, which moved to extend unemployment benefits during the deep recession. There was no opposition in the Senate to this bill; it would ultimately pass 98–0 in November 2009. But before then, minority Republicans mounted two filibusters, both on the motion to proceed to debate the bill and on its final passage. Each filibuster took two days before the Senate could bring up the cloture motion, and then another thirty hours each for postcloture debate. The senators adopted the first cloture motion 87–13; the second, 97–1.[10] A bill that should have zipped through in a day or two at most took four weeks, including seven days of floor time, to be enacted.

Then there was the case of another slam dunk, H.R. 627, the Credit Cardholders' Bill of Rights Act. Its purpose was, among other things, to limit usurious interest rates and exorbitant hidden charges. This bill ended up with only one cloture vote, after the filibuster on the motion to proceed was withdrawn. The cloture motion on passage of the bill sailed through on a vote of 92–2, and the bill passed by a 90–5 vote.[11] But again, the clog in the process due to the filibuster threats and Rule XXII meant weeks of delay and seven days of floor time.

Our final example is the Fraud Enforcement and Recovery Act, S. 386, designed to increase criminal penalties for mortgage and securities fraud, among others. Once again, another futile filibuster, with cloture successfully invoked on final passage. The vote on the cloture motion was 84–4, on final passage, 92–4. This act took six days of floor time.[12]

These three noncontroversial bills passed with overwhelming majorities. A mere decade ago, they would have taken a grand total of three or four days to pass, including amendments. Now they take twenty days of precious and limited floor time, with the largest portion spent not on debating the merits of the bills or working intensively to improve them via substantive amendments, but on making action or progress on other bills more cumbersome and difficult. Because Rule XXII allows thirty hours of debate after cloture is successful, and because the rule does not require senators to actually be on the floor debating, Republicans have been able to insist on using the full thirty hours just to draw things out, not to debate a relevant issue. During those thirty hours, nothing of substance happens. Often, it's just a mind-numbing calling of the roll after a senator notes the absence of a quorum—over and over again. This fits neither the intent of the rule nor the long-standing norms of the institution about what to do once a side has lost in votes on the floor—namely, accept defeat and move on to the next issue.

Executive and Judicial Appointments

In another unfortunate use of the filibuster, senators have increasingly employed it to cripple presidents' ability to fill executive and judicial branch positions.

Consider President Obama's nomination of Judge Barbara Milano Keenan to the U.S. Court of Appeals for the Fourth Circuit. Judge Keenan's qualifications were impeccable; as a judge on Virginia's Supreme Court, she was widely praised. But her confirmation in March 2011 was subject to a filibuster and a cloture motion that passed 99–0, followed by a similar 99–0 confirmation vote. In the case of Judge Keenan, her confirmation occurred a full 169 days after her nomination, and 124 days after the Judiciary Committee unanimously reported her nomination to the floor.[13] By our estimate, a process that the Senate could have handled in a few weeks, from formal nomination to committee hearing to confirmation, took almost half a year and wasted dozens of hours of floor time.

At least Judge Keenan's nomination eventually made it to the floor. Senators have increasingly used holds, their ability to block consideration of a nominee indefinitely, as a broader partisan weapon to keep presidents from filling key positions, including many qualified and usually noncontroversial nominees.[14] Here the focus, and damage, has been mainly on appellate judicial nominations (numbering roughly twenty-five to fifty per Congress) and the 400 or so Senate-confirmed senior positions in cabinet departments and executive agencies (excluding ambassadors) that serve at the pleasure of the president. In the case of the former, the confirmation process since the Clinton era has become increasingly prolonged and contentious. The confirmation rate of presidential circuit court appointments has plummeted from above 90 percent in the late 1970s and early 1980s to around 50 percent in recent years.

A particularly acrimonious confrontation over the delay by Democrats of several of President George W. Bush's judicial nominations in 2005 led then Majority Leader Bill Frist to threaten use of the so-called "nuclear option"—a ruling from the chair sustained by a simple majority of senators to establish that the Constitution required the Senate to vote up or down on every judicial nomination (effectively, cloture by simple majority). Before the arrival of Frist's deadline for breaking the impasse, a group of fourteen senators (seven Democrats and seven Republicans) reached an informal pact to oppose Frist's "reform-by-ruling" while denying Democrats the ability to filibuster several of the pending nominations. This defused the immediate situation but did little to alter the long-run trajectory of the judicial confirmation process.

In earlier decades, senators almost always gave great leeway to presidents in picking judges, with disputes being the exception, not the rule, and most nominees being chosen because of experience and qualifications and with less regard for ideological purity. The Supreme Court through most of the twentieth century, up through the 1960s and into the 1970s, had many members who had served in elective office. Many, like Earl Warren or Hugo Black, had not been judges before their appointments. Often, as with Warren, their judicial opinions were in no way predictable from their previous jobs or statements. But as the political process became more polarized in the 1970s, 1980s, and beyond, judicial appointments also became more ideological and polarized, and more choices for the Supreme Court were appeals court judges, who had a lengthy record that made their likely opinions predictable going forward.

Lifetime appointments and the new, highly ideological stakes provided senators ample incentives to use holds and silent filibusters to prevent a majority of their colleagues from acting on judicial nominations, both to block those with different ideologies and to keep slots vacant until the presidency moves into their party's hands. Along the way, judicial confirmations have become increasingly politicized, and delays in confirming appellate judges have led to increased vacancy rates that have produced longer case-processing times and growing caseloads per judge on federal dockets.

The process became acute when Republican majorities in the Senate during the Clinton presidency blocked not just liberals but moderate nominees for judicial posts. Democrats applied it in turn, albeit less aggressively, during the Bush presidency. But the process ratcheted up again with President Obama, and the conflict over appellate judges began to spill over to district court appointments, which are beginning to produce similarly low rates of confirmation. The current administration worsened its own problem with inexplicable delays at the beginning of Obama's presidency in nominating candidates to fill a large number of judicial vacancies. But the senators' aggressive move to use the hold and threat of filibuster to keep judicial vacancies open, with the hope that the slots will be available for the next president to fill, is the key phenomenon here.

Even more disconcerting has been the distortion of the confirmation process for executive nominees; the more it has become a political weapon, the less effectively presidents have been able to staff their administrations and run the government. As political scientist G. Calvin Mackenzie testified to the Senate Rules Committee in 2011, "We have in Washington today a presidential appointment process that is a less efficient and less effective mechanism for staffing the senior levels of government than its counterparts in any other industrialized democracy."[15] Some of the problem rests with administrations' increasingly sclerotic nomination process. In an effort to do more thorough background checks to avoid ethical embarrassments, they are taking much more time vetting potential nominees before formally choosing them.

But the trends over the last four administrations place an increasing responsibility for delays on the Senate. The average time the Senate took to confirm nominees in the first year of new administrations has steadily increased (from 51.5 days under George H. W. Bush to 60.8 days under Barack Obama), while the percentage of presidential nominations it confirmed by the end of the first year declined (from 80.1 percent under George H. W. Bush to 64.4 percent under Barack Obama).[16] These discouraging statistics actually understate the problem. The Senate usually confirms cabinet secretaries within a couple of weeks, while taking on average almost three months for top non-cabinet agency officials. The Senate has subjected some nominees to much more extended delays, leaving critical positions unfilled for much or all of a president's first year in office. The effects reverberate: citizens offering to serve their country, often at significant personal and financial cost, are forced to put their personal lives on hold for many months. With the stress this puts on their careers, marriages, and children, will really talented people remain willing to subject themselves to such indignity? The government that we want to be more effective is crippled. Some cabinet secretaries have to manage with only skeleton senior staffs; a number, in office temporarily through recess appointments, have lacked the empowerment that comes with Senate confirmation. Recent administrations have many horror stories associated with the absence of timely confirmation of its top executives. And again, the amount of wasted time that the Senate could spend doing more productive things boggles the mind.

As Jonathan Cohn of *The New Republic* put it,

True, the constitution gives the Senate the power to "advise and consent" on executive branch appointments. And from the early days of the republic through the end of the 19th Century, the Senate and president fought regularly over the precise boundaries of that power—most famously when the Reconstruction Congress passed a law forbidding then President Andrew Johnson from removing a cabinet official without congressional permission. It was his decision to flout that law that drew impeachment and, very nearly, his removal from office.

But since that time the Senate has deferred more to the president on appointments, partly on the theory that a modern society needs a president who could staff the executive branch with like-minded officials. Although senators have frequently raised substantive and ideological objections to nominees, explicitly or implicitly, they did not engage in such wholesale, blanket opposition to appointments based (explicitly or even implicitly) on governing philosophy. As the Senate's own website confirms, the Senate voted down nominations "only in the most blatant instances of unsuitability." The obvious exception has been judicial appointments. But even those have increased dramatically in the last few years and, besides, those are lifetime appointments to an entirely separate branch of government.

What makes this ideological policing even more pernicious is the fact that it's policing by a minority.[17]

A few recent examples drive home the cost of this folly. In mid- to late 2009, in the midst of the financial meltdown when critical decisions had to be made on the implementation of the Troubled Asset Relief Program (TARP), the Treasury Department had nominees for a slew of high-ranking policy positions twisting in the wind awaiting Senate confirmation. Treasury Secretary Tim Geithner had no deputy secretary, undersecretary for international affairs, undersecretary for domestic finance, assistant secretary for tax policy, assistant secretary for financial markets, assistant secretary for financial stability, and assistant secretary for legislative affairs. And the Senate has delayed other economy-related positions, some for as long as a year or more, at a time when the economy continues to struggle. Testifying in 2011 before the Senate Banking Committee, Sheila Bair, the outgoing chairwoman of the Federal Deposit Insurance Corporation (FDIC), a key figure in the ongoing banking crisis, warned of significant risk to the financial system posed by the failure to approve qualified candidates for posts at the FDIC, Treasury, and Federal Housing Finance Agency—not to mention the new Consumer Financial Protection Bureau.

Early in the Obama administration, there was a long list of other critical positions with urgent responsibilities that waited for months without a vote in the Senate to fill them. They included the commissioner of U.S. Customs and Border Protection, director of the Transportation Security Administration, head of the National Highway Traffic Safety Administration, and director of the Centers for Medicare and Medicaid Services (more about this later). While in some of these instances, the delays occurred for legitimate reasons, in the overwhelming majority, they came down to either ideological and partisan battles in the Senate or the personal agendas and vendettas of individual senators. In every instance, the senators ignored the need to put people in place to run agencies and solve national problems.

Currently, because most holds remain secret at the request of individual senators, there is no foolproof way we can discern how many nominations are subject to holds. We can, however, examine the list of nominations that committees have approved and placed on the Senate executive calendar. We presume that absent a hold or other signal of a filibuster, the Majority Leader will move expeditiously to call up these nominations. Not long ago, it was rare that nominees would linger on the list of pending confirmation for days, weeks, and months. On Memorial Day, 2002, during George W. Bush's administration, thirteen nominations were pending on the executive calendar. Eight years later, under Obama, the number was 108.[18]

The New Nullification

Republicans' efforts in the tacit cause of partisan rivalry to block the confirmation of nominees—to embarrass the president and hobble his ability to run the executive branch—are troubling enough. But the new strategy has an additional, even more disturbing element: *blocking nominations, even while acknowledging the competence and integrity of the nominees, to prevent the legitimate implementation of laws on the books.* In many cases, if no person is running an agency charged with enforcing a law, the agency can't easily implement or enforce the law; career bureaucrats are reluctant to make critical decisions without the imprimatur of the presidential appointee who should be running the agency. We call this—together with other tactics, including repeal of just-enacted statutes, coordinated challenges to their constitutionality, and denial of funds for implementation—the new nullification, in reference to the pre–Civil War theory in Southern states that a state could ignore or nullify a federal law it unilaterally viewed as unconstitutional.

President Obama's nomination of Donald Berwick to run the Centers for Medicare and Medicaid Services, the agency primarily responsible for implementing the Affordable Care Act, or health-care reform, may have started the trend. While some during

Berwick's confirmation hearing made charges questioning his judgment in such areas as the effectiveness of Britain's health-care system, no one questioned his qualifications or integrity. But Republican Senate leaders threatened to filibuster his nomination, forcing President Obama to make Berwick a recess appointee with a limited term and with significantly limited clout compared to Senate-confirmed administrators. A widely respected scholar and practitioner whose career had been focused on ways to reduce health-care costs without harming patients, Berwick was a nearly ideal choice for the job. There is no plausible reason for the threats of filibuster other than the Republicans' attempt to hobble the new health-care program. When Berwick announced his resignation right before the end of his recess appointment, the *Daily Caller*, a conservative website, wrote, "Earlier this year, 42 Republican senators promised to block Berwick's confirmation. Their success in preventing Berwick's appointment represents another blow to the president's health care law—Berwick was an important actor in introducing its reforms."[19] The result has effectively retarded or bollixed up the implementation of a law enacted by elected officials.

The blocking strategy continued with Peter Diamond, a Nobel Prize–winning economist at MIT, nominated for a seat on the Federal Reserve Board, who was also stymied by a party-led filibuster. Then, even more troubling, the Senate Republican leaders declared that they would block confirmation of *any* nominee, no matter how distinguished or qualified, to head the Consumer Financial Protection Bureau (CFPB) created by the Dodd-Frank financial regulation reform act, unless the administration agreed to change the structure of the agency specified in the law. Having lost that legislative battle when the Dodd-Frank bill was enacted, they now insisted that a key provision be altered before they would allow the CFPB to exercise its statutory authority. Republicans used the threat of filibuster to block Elizabeth Warren, a Harvard Law School professor and the intellectual parent of the CFPB, from consideration for the position. So President Obama turned to Richard Cordray, a former Ohio attorney general. At his confirmation hearing in July 2011, Republicans on the Senate Banking Committee praised his background, character, qualifications, and family, before making it abundantly clear that he would not be confirmed because they do not like the law. Then, adopting and expanding a practice initiated by Majority Leader Reid at the end of the Bush administration, Republicans refused to allow the Congress to recess at the end of 2011. They insisted on a series of "pro forma" sessions every three days, with only a single member present, to deny the president the ability to make any recess appointments. President Obama, drawing on legal advice first offered by the Office of Legal Counsel in the Bush administration and reinforced by his own legal advisors, insisted that his constitutional authority to make recess appointments could not be abrogated by such means and appointed Cordray to head the CFPB, albeit with a shorter duration and lesser legitimacy than a regular Senate confirmation would provide.

Whether lawmakers like or dislike laws, they are under oath to carry them out. They can move, under their Article 1 powers, to repeal the laws, amend the laws, or even cut off funding for them, subject to the checks and balances otherwise in the Constitution. And, of course, they are free to run in the next election against those laws. But to use the hold and filibuster to undermine laws on the books from being implemented is an underhanded tactic, one reflecting, in our view, the increasing dysfunction of a parliamentary-style minority party distorting the rules and norms of the Senate to accomplish its ideological and partisan ends.

Is It Really As Bad As It Looks?

Holds, filibusters, and other delay and obstruction tactics have been around since the beginning of the republic. But as we look at the panoply of tactics and techniques for throwing wrenches and grenades into the regular order of the policy process, which the new and old media's outside agitation encourages and even incites, we do not see business as usual. The target is no longer an individual judge or cabinet member hated for a real or imagined ideological leaning. The pathologies we've identified, old and new, provide incontrovertible evidence of people who have become more loyal to party than to country. As a result, the political system has become grievously hobbled at a time when the country faces unusually serious challenges and grave threats.

The single-minded focus on scoring political points over solving problems, escalating over the last several decades, has reached a level of such intensity and bitterness that the government seems incapable of taking and sustaining public decisions responsive to the existential challenges facing the country. The public may still revere the Constitution and support the system of government that it shaped, but this is more a measure of patriotism—love of country and pride in being an American—than of satisfaction with how it is working in practice. All of the boastful talk of American exceptionalism cannot obscure the growing sense that the country is squandering its economic future and putting itself at risk because of an inability to govern effectively. This is a time of immense economic peril, with the global economy at risk, sustained unemployment that can hollow out the work force in the future, a lack of any long-term fiscal policy that can be enacted, and the need for action in areas from climate change to immigration.

The Problem Is Mismatch

We believe a fundamental problem is the mismatch between parliamentary-style political parties—ideologically polarized, internally unified, vehemently oppositional, and politically strategic—that has emerged in recent years and a separation-of-powers system that makes it extremely difficult for majorities to work their will. Students of comparative politics have demonstrated that the American policy-making system of checks and balances and separation of powers has more structural impediments to action than any other major democracy.[20] Now there are additional incentives for obstruction in that policy-making process. Witness the Republicans' immense electoral success in 2010 after voting in unison against virtually every Obama initiative and priority, and making each vote and enactment contentious and excruciating, followed by major efforts to delegitimize the result. And because of the partisan nature of much of the media and the reflexive tendency of many in the mainstream press to use false equivalence to explain outcomes, it becomes much easier for a minority, in this case the Republicans, to use filibusters, holds, and other techniques to obstruct. The status quo bias of the constitutional system becomes magnified under dysfunction and creates a take-no-prisoners political dynamic that gives new meaning to the late Daniel Patrick Moynihan's concept of "defining deviancy down."[21]

An American Insurgency

The dysfunction that arises from the incompatibility of the U.S. constitutional system with parliamentary-type parties is compounded by the asymmetric polarization of those parties. Today's

Republican Party, as we noted at the beginning of the book, is an insurgent outlier. It has become ideologically extreme; contemptuous of the inherited social and economic policy regime; scornful of compromise; unpersuaded by conventional understanding of facts, evidence, and science; and dismissive of the legitimacy of its political opposition, all but declaring war on the government. The Democratic Party, while no paragon of civic virtue, is more ideologically centered and diverse, protective of the government's role as it developed over the course of the last century, open to incremental changes in policy fashioned through bargaining with the Republicans, and less disposed to or adept at take-no-prisoners conflict between the parties. This asymmetry between the parties, which journalists and scholars often brush aside or whitewash in a quest for "balance," constitutes a huge obstacle to effective governance.

Bringing the Republican Party back into the mainstream of American politics and policy and return to a more regular, problem-solving orientation for both parties would go a long way toward reducing the dysfunctionality of American politics. Yet it would not magically return America and the American political system to a golden era. The other changes we have begun to outline, including the profound changes in the mass media, the coarsening of American culture, the populist distrust of nearly all leaders except those in the military, and the insidious and destructive role of money in politics and policy making, would still be in place, making problem solving all the more vexing. As we continue to analyze the impact of this dysfunction, we will focus on new ways to ameliorate these broader problems as well.

PART II

What to Do About It

Bromides to Avoid

I f our summary of the scope, seriousness, and roots of America's dysfunctional politics is on target, then remedies for healing and renewing the political system should be consistent with this diagnosis. Before proceeding to identify those strategies for change, we need to explain how many highly visible responses for overcoming these difficulties are inconsistent with our diagnosis. In our view, they offer little source of comfort or promise of remediation.

The American Political System Will Correct Itself

The first response is a wholesale rejection of the conventional wisdom that the political system is dangerously broken. Such a charge, the argument goes, lacks a proper appreciation of the magnitude of the problems confronting the country in the wake of the global financial crisis and Great Recession, the struggles of worldwide democracies to deal effectively with comparable problems, the similar patterns of subpar performance and political dysfunction that America has overcome in the past, and the unrecognized strengths of the U.S. constitutional system in adapting to new circumstances and making self-corrections.

This defense of the current system reflects the considered judgment of many who have devoted their professional lives to the study of American political history. They are well aware of the turbulent times, pitched battles between contending forces, delays in responding to crises, and unseemly machinations within the chambers of Congress the country has experienced throughout its history. For many years, we considered ourselves kindred spirits. Polarized parties are not a novel feature of American politics. The years surrounding the War of 1812, the lead-up to the Civil War, and the post-Reconstruction period around the turn of the century featured intense partisanship and governmental dysfunction. Reconciling strongly held competing views and clashing interests is a difficult and messy process, one that naturally attracts public opprobrium. Polarized parties multiply the degree of difficulty in navigating a constitutional system that separates power and checks and balances its exercise. Nonetheless, with the striking exception of the Civil War, even periods of partisan polarization have proven manageable, as voters and politicians slowly and painfully grappled with the problems of American democracy and dealt with the challenges of their times.

Scholars of contemporary American politics have defended the durability and adaptability of the constitutional system, especially those who specialize in the study of Congress. The eminent Yale political scientist David R. Mayhew provides a good example. In his 2005 book *Divided We Govern*, Mayhew responded to critics who bemoaned the gridlock in divided party government, finding that legislative productivity—measured by significant laws enacted and congressional investigations conducted—did not differ significantly between unified and divided party governments from 1946 to 2002.[1] To be sure, his findings are not undisputed. Sarah Binder, an expert on Congress at the Brookings Institution, mounted a powerful response by presenting evidence in support of her argument that divided control of government increases the stalemate in Congress.[2]

In Mayhew's 2011 book, *Partisan Balance: Why Political Parties Don't Kill the U.S. Constitutional System*, he argues that the unique and peculiar systems responsible for the election of the president, Senate, and House have over the last sixty years produced largely majoritarian outcomes, "microcosms of the national electorate" that render each of the three institutions both representative and functional and with no significant bias favoring one party over the other.[3] He also examines the success rates in Congress of Democratic and Republican presidents' domestic policy proposals during their first two years in the White House. Here too what he discovers is reassuring: a healthy harvest for presidents of roughly 60 percent, the same under unified and divided governments, and only modest and explainable differences between Republicans and Democrats. He also surprisingly finds no confirmation of the widespread view that the filibuster-empowered Senate is largely responsible for the defeat of presidential proposals. More generally, Mayhew finds little evidence that anti-majoritarian procedures in either the House or the Senate prevented presidents from garnering approval of proposals that a majority of their members favored.

Mayhew concludes that "most of the imbalances I have observed in this work have *not* been major, permanent systemic problems. More precisely, at least during recent generations, many alleged problems have proven to be nonexistent, short-term, limited, tolerable, or correctable."[4] Americans, he argues, look for change at the next election rather than through institutional fixes or constitutional reform. And, presumably, that option is sufficient both to assuage their concerns and to produce policy-making responses within the range of sufficiency and public acceptability.

Mayhew's argument is a comforting reminder of how, over many years, unlovely political processes and institutions have represented majority sentiment, adapted to changing contexts, grappled with serious problems, overcome policy impasses, and produced more of a "shrug" from the public than demands for structural change. The reminder is perhaps too comforting. We can't help but notice the poor fit of the first three years of the Obama presidency with Mayhew's story of popular sovereignty and institutional self-correction. Consider the following elements of the first three years:

- Sharply asymmetric polarization, with an insurgent Republican party far from the mainstream of American politics.
- The virtual disappearance of regular order in Congress.
- The widespread denial of the elected president's legitimacy.
- An unbending opposition-party strategy of obstructing, demonizing, and nullifying presidential initiatives, accomplishments, and appointments during economic crisis.
- Following a decisive public embrace of change in the 2010 elections, a dramatic decline in legislative productivity from the unified 111th Congress to the divided 112th.

- The hostage taking of the full faith and credit of the United States.

- The first-ever downgrade of U.S. securities.

- Nonnegotiable demands producing gridlock on issues of prime importance, including economic recovery and deficits and debt.

- Record low levels of public approval of Congress, trust in government, and confidence in the capacity of political leaders and institutions to deal with pressing problems.

- A large majority believing that dire economic conditions will not improve.

We hope Mayhew is right and that this difficult patch will prove to be routine, short term and self-correcting, or at least easily correctible. But we doubt it. These perilous times and the political responses to them are qualitatively different from what we have seen before. There is no guarantee that the country's troubles will be short-lived and the political system self-correcting. Indeed, the magnitude of the problems in the wake of the most serious economic crisis since the 1930s and the difficulty other democracies are experiencing in trying to mitigate its devastating effects should strengthen America's resolve to fix its dysfunctional politics.

Third Party to the Rescue

For those fed up with the political order, another logical but ill-considered response is the third-party candidate. In recent decades, Ross Perot, John Anderson, and George Wallace have served that purpose, though only Wallace managed to win any electoral votes. Third-party or independent presidential candidates often arise to fill a vacuum in the structure of the major party competition, but never themselves come close to occupying the White House.[5] *New York Times* columnist Thomas Friedman[6] and the *Washington Post*'s Matt Miller[7] have each written a series of articles that lay out their case for an independent presidential candidate. That person would mobilize the "radical center," a large segment of the public they see as fed up with polarized partisan politics and yearning for pragmatic, problem-solving leaders who will set aside politics and enact responsible policies to solve the nation's massive problems. Their preferred vehicle for achieving this objective is Americans Elect, a new 501(c)4 organization that policy and business entrepreneur Peter Ackerman created. Ackerman hopes to attract millions of registered voters in nominating an independent presidential candidate via an Internet-based convention.[8]

We don't question Friedman's and Miller's policy goals, which they see as the most promising means of meeting the long-term challenges before the country. We do, however, question their political acuity, both the assumptions behind their analysis and their failure to anticipate the damaging, counterproductive consequences that could result from such an effort.

Let's start with their readings of public opinion. They and many others supporting an independent or third-party movement believe that a large majority of Americans have contempt for the major parties and are clustered in the political center. Courageous political leaders speaking honest truths can persuade them to embrace enlightened proposals to tax carbon; cut entitlements; make critical public investments in education, scientific research, infrastructure, and clean energy; reduce or eliminate tax credits and deductions while lowering rates; and generate new revenues sufficient to drastically reduce deficits and stabilize public debt.

The reality, alas, suggests otherwise. While sizable majorities of survey respondents typically voice antiparty sentiments in response to pollsters' questions, roughly 90 percent of voters identify with or lean to one of the two major parties. Most self-identified independents are closet partisans.[9] Moreover, these voters view the political and policy worlds through their partisan lenses and loyally support their party's candidates at the polls. As we discussed earlier, the public was not immune to the polarizing dynamic that created the wide gulf between the two parties over the last several decades. Pure independents or swing voters make up barely a tenth of the electorate, and their presumed centrism or pragmatism in most cases reflects political disengagement and a lack of knowledge about the parties, candidates, or policy choices, rather than a considered position in the center. They are classic referendum voters: when times are bad, their instinct is to throw the bums out, not to carefully attribute responsibility or parse alternatives.[10]

There is simply no reliable evidence to support the belief that voters would flock to a straight-talking, centrist, independent, or third-party candidate articulating the favored policies of Friedman, Miller, or countless other individuals advocating support of nonpartisan or bipartisan initiatives. Consensus does not exist and is not easily built, and a candidate independent of the two parties cannot sweep away the political and institutional obstacles to enacting "responsible" policies. Candidates have to contest differences in values, interests, public philosophies, and policies directly in the electoral arena, not submerge them in a nonpartisan feel-good centrism. Parties have always played and will continue to play a vital role in all democracies, America's included, in framing choices for voters and in organizing governments to act on their collective decisions. We must address the flaws in the electoral system and in the rules and procedures of political institutions directly, so the flaws are not end-run by a chimerical knight on a white horse.

This isn't to say there isn't a meaningful role for independent presidential candidates; indeed, some have effectively used the bully pulpit in a visible presidential campaign to raise the profile of an important issue, as Ross Perot did in 1992 on the issue of deficits and debt. His message resonated with many voters. The next year, an economic plan that the new president, Bill Clinton, crafted paid more attention to deficits than his campaign plan had and was enacted by Congress. Economic experts subsequently recognized it as a huge contributor to the budget surpluses that followed. But Perot's persuasiveness in the campaign did not convince a single Republican in either house of Congress to vote for Bill Clinton's economic plan, which eventually limped home by a single vote in each chamber. And we now look back on that time as less partisan and less polarized than now.

Another flaw in the reasoning of those who advance an independent or third-party presidential candidate comes back to a failure to acknowledge the asymmetry of the two parties. During his first term, Barack Obama favored most of the policies embraced by those longing for a "grand bargain," to stimulate the economy in the short run and deal with the long-term deficits. Every Republican candidate for president in 2012 and every leader in Congress rejected those policies. Obama is the kind of centrist candidate that champions of a third-party presidential candidate seek. One of their complaints is with his failure to explicitly embrace proposals such as the recommendations of the Simpson-Bowles deficit-reduction commission or a carbon tax that might form the basis of a grand bargain including tax reform. But this is simply disagreement over tactics and timing. Given unified Republican opposition to anything the president publicly supports, we suspect Obama has the better of the argument. Recall the memo we cited from a senior Republican Senate aide after Obama reacted warmly to the Senate "Gang of Six" deficit-reduction plan, saying in effect, "if he is for it, we will kill it."

Advocates of a third-party candidate like Miller and Friedman also complain about Obama's failure to deliver on the policies they espouse. But here the complaint is misdirected. Better to generate public pressure on the GOP to break their lockstep opposition to Obama's entire agenda, abandon their no-new-taxes pledge, and change the Senate filibuster rule to reduce its new and regularized obstructionist role than to cling to a false equivalence between the parties and blame them equally for policy failure. Those advocating a third-party or independent presidential candidate fail to offer any plausible scenario of how such a successful candidate could govern effectively, given the state of the parties in Congress and the supermajority hurdles in the Senate.

This brings us to the potential dangers of pursuing an independent or third-party strategy. Without a system of runoff elections or ranked preferences, a third-party candidate could well produce an outcome a majority of voters would not favor and become more of a spoiler than anything else. In 2012, a centrist third-party candidate would be more likely to siphon votes from Obama, given the policies he has supported and those the Republican candidates espouse. When you have two centrist candidates running against one conservative, the advantage will clearly go to the latter, even though the conservative's positions will be less likely in line with the majority.

Americans Elect's goals of using the Internet to provide millions of registered voters an opportunity to participate directly in the nomination of a presidential ticket seem well intentioned. We have no doubt that Peter Ackerman and his son Elliot, who is running Americans Elect, are honorable in their motives. But the more we look at the behavior of this nascent organization, the more questions we have. For an organization dedicated to accountability and transparency, its decision to switch from a 527 political organization to a 501(c)4 social welfare organization whose donors are not subject to disclosure through the Federal Election Commission (FEC) raises serious questions. A deliberate move to hide the identity of donors is not a commendable path for a "reformist" organization.

Americans Elect's board member and primary source of public opinion data, Douglas Schoen, has collaborated with another estranged Democrat, Patrick Caddell, in a series of columns in the *Wall Street Journal* and pronouncements on Fox News that are harshly (and, in our view, inaccurately) critical of Obama, calling into question the even-handedness of American Elect's leadership. Even assuming the best of intentions, the organization is not constituted to produce a responsible and accountable outcome. It suffers from a serious democratic deficit, in which founding members and self-appointed committees play a disproportionate role in its governance.[11] Moreover, the design of the nomination process makes it exceedingly vulnerable to efforts by other candidates and their well-heeled donors to influence the choice of a nominee. We don't see anything to prevent hundreds of thousands or millions of Democratic and Republican activists, with no intention of supporting an independent candidate in the general election, from becoming "delegates" for Americans Elect and casting their Internet ballots strategically to advance their party's interest.

Whatever the mechanism for nominating an independent or third-party presidential candidate, this solution to dysfunctional politics would actually reduce the public's ability to resolve a critical debate shaping the country's future. A plurality, not a majority, of voters would likely determine the identity of the next president (if the country is fortunate to avoid the horrors of an election by the House of Representatives, where each state's delegation would cast a single vote for president, making Alaska, South Dakota, and Wyoming combined three times as powerful as California). The victorious ticket would have little basis in electoral mandate or support in Congress to lead the country forward.

Faced with some of the criticism, the *Post*'s Miller has proposed focusing the efforts of this movement on electing members of Congress—going into the swing districts, ones where either party has a shot at victory, and empowering independents to prevail enough to create a new centrist caucus in the House.[12] Most of the target districts actually happen to be ones where the remaining moderate Blue Dog Democrats either have been elected or have a chance of victory against arch-conservative Republicans. This movement would be far more likely to drain votes from centrist, center-left, or center-right Democratic candidates or incumbents and provide more victories for extreme Republicans—or in at least a few instances harm center-right or right-center Republicans to elect very liberal Democrats—than to accomplish the desired goals.

A Constitutional Amendment to Balance the Budget

Enshrining a requirement for an annual balanced budget in the Constitution is a faulty response to overcoming America's dysfunctional politics, although it is a centerpiece of congressional Republicans' plans to deal with deficits and debt and endorsed by all the candidates seeking the GOP presidential nomination. Yes, some version of this amendment is part of forty-nine state constitutions. Yes, more than three-quarters of the public consistently supports its addition to the federal constitution. Yes, federal budget deficits have reached record levels in the past several years, and public debt as a share of the total economy is on a course to threaten the country's financial integrity. And yes, the regular congressional budget process during this period of time has only nibbled at the edges of the problem in spite of its seriousness.

The 2011 House Republican plan to "Cut, Cap and Balance" the federal budget requires that federal spending be capped over ten years at 19.9 percent of GDP and makes it contingent on passage of a constitutional amendment, which requires spending and revenues to be balanced and a two-thirds majority in both the House and Senate to approve any increase in taxes and in the debt ceiling. Republicans brought the plan up for a vote in the House and intend to do so again. Most Republican presidential candidates have endorsed it.

It is not the only balanced budget amendment out there. The amendment that most House Republicans and every Senate Republican have endorsed is even more draconian. It would cap spending at 18 percent of GDP, but based on the previous year's GDP, meaning, according to Republican economist Donald Marron, a cap of 16.7 percent of GDP in federal spending.[13] This amendment, if added to the Constitution, would require drastic cuts in every area of spending, from health research to food safety to defense and homeland security to Medicare and Social Security, taking America's social policy back to pre–New Deal territory. The caps could be overcome only via a formal declaration of war or when Congress recognizes a military conflict is underway, and any increased spending over the cap would have to be applied to the military action.

So what's the problem with a balanced budget amendment? The huge cuts in federal spending and/or increases in taxes would be required immediately following ratification. The super-majority requirement for tax increases makes it highly likely that only spending cuts would be on the table. The public that supports a balanced budget amendment has no idea that these cuts are perforce part of the deal. By way of comparison, the ambitious, conservative budget resolution crafted by Budget Committee Chairman Paul Ryan and approved by House Republicans, which includes deep cuts in discretionary domestic spending and a major restructuring of the Medicare and Medicaid programs, would not reach a balance for decades.

If the amendment were ratified quickly, these deep cuts would be made at a time in which the economy remains at risk of a double-dip recession. Such an austerity program would likely further slow economic activity, diminish federal revenues, and increase the deficit rather than balance the budget. This underscores the importance of fiscal flexibility over the course of a business cycle, whether by automatic stabilizers such as unemployment benefits or discrete steps by Congress, to prevent economic downturns from spiraling into extended recessions or depressions. Fiscal flexibility is especially critical in a federal system in which states are obligated to balance their budgets. The states' balanced budget requirements guarantee substantial fiscal drag during a downturn because they require procyclical spending cuts and tax increases at the most inopportune times, leaving the federal government to provide that countercyclical balance. A modern economy must have the capacity to use deficits and debt strategically for its well-being.

Of course, this assumes that Congress could or would successfully implement a balanced-budget constitutional amendment.

The odds of that happening? Zilch. There is a reason many politicians are much more eager to support a constitutional amendment than specific steps to balance the budget. Supporting the amendment route allows them to proclaim their fiscal virtue with little chance of having it tested. As far as the public is concerned, it means cutting waste, fraud, and abuse while eliminating unspecified (but surely worthless) governmental programs. If the amendment were ratified and Congress moved to implement it, a hue and cry from their constituents would surely follow. Where will the congressional majorities to cut these programs come from? How about the supermajorities to raise taxes? Our guess is that neither would materialize. That means presidential and congressional gimmicks to move parts of federal spending off budget (as has occurred in the states), lawsuits against Congress, federal courts assuming the power of the purse, and continuing artificial crises with the debt limit and threat of default, together serving mainly to reinforce and extend dysfunctional politics, not to ameliorate it.

In the past, America has run up deficits and increased debt during times of war and economic distress, and then managed to keep that debt from burdening the country as temporary spending increases receded and the economy grew at a healthy pace. After deficits increased to worrisome levels in the 1980s, President Reagan signed a number of bills to scale back part of his large tax cuts, and then President George H. W. Bush agreed in 1990 to a substantial deficit-reduction package that included rate increases for high-income households. The latter package garnered Bush only a handful of Republican votes in the House; he cut the deal with the majority Democrats and earned the enmity of the GOP. President Clinton was persuaded to shift from his campaign call for middle-class tax cuts to a deficit-reduction package similar in size and scope to that of Bush. As we noted earlier, it barely passed Congress in 1993 under the protection of reconciliation, a budget-related procedure that prevents Senate filibusters by limiting the time for debate, without a single Republican vote in the House or Senate. Those two plans had much to do with the remarkable if short-lived era of budget balance and surpluses that ended abruptly with the George W. Bush presidency.

During this decade-long struggle to contain growing deficits, Congress tried a number of institutional fixes to grapple with the problem. What didn't work were mechanisms that directly targeted the size of budget deficits. These deficits were determined at least as much by the state of the economy as by policy decisions. What did work were caps on discretionary spending and a pay-as-you-go rule that required any reductions in taxes or increases in mandatory spending (i.e., entitlements) be balanced with some combinations of tax increases and mandatory spending cuts. The PAYGO rule, implemented as part of that 1990 budget agreement, was impressively successful at building in budget discipline.

Starting in the mid-1990s and continuing through the decade, strong economic growth and higher marginal tax rates produced a surge in federal revenues and a dramatic decline in the size of the deficit. Spending during these years was restrained. The 1997 Balanced Budget Act (and its companion Taxpayer Relief Act), enacted under a divided party government, contributed relatively little to the movement toward a balanced budget. Its most significant components—a new Children's Health Insurance Program and a reduction in the capital gains tax rate—moved in the opposite direction. And its biggest spending cut—reducing reimbursement of physicians under Medicare—was unrealistic and has never taken effect; each year Congress passes a "doc fix" to prevent that from happening. Before this agreement was implemented, the budget had already made the transition from deficit to surplus.[14]

Clinton bequeathed to President George W. Bush a substantial budget surplus, one expected to total $4 trillion over the next decade. The PAYGO statute expired in 2002, and Republicans refused to continue it. (When Democrats recaptured the majority in the House in 2007, they reinstated a version of PAYGO as a rule. Republicans repealed it when they returned to power in 2011, implementing instead a rule they call CUTGO, meaning any spending increase would have to be offset by a spending cut, but leaving any tax cuts exempt from offsets.)

Fretting that the national debt would be paid off and budget surpluses perforce invested in purchasing shares in private companies, Federal Reserve Chairman Alan Greenspan supported Bush's proposals for large tax cuts.[15] (A decade later, in the face of crushing deficits, he urged that they be allowed to expire.) The tax cuts in 2001 and 2003, the addition of a prescription drug benefit to Medicare, wars in Afghanistan and Iraq, a massive buildup of homeland security following the terrorist attacks of September 11, and mediocre economic growth turned those surpluses into deficits. Economist Bruce Bartlett, who served in the Reagan administration, wrote that the Bush tax cuts did not provide offsetting economic growth; in fact, "real GDP growth peaked at 3.6 percent in 2004 before fading rapidly. Even before the crisis hit, real GDP was growing less than 2 percent a year."[16]

In the decade after the Bush tax cuts, growth was the lowest it had been in any decade since World War II. A Congressional Budget Office report said the tax cuts reduced revenue over the ten years between 2001 and 2011 by at least $2.9 trillion below what it would have been, while less than expected growth reduced revenue by another $3.5 trillion. Bartlett commented, "Spending was $5.6 trillion higher than the CBO anticipated for a total fiscal turnaround of $12 trillion. That is how a $6 trillion projected surplus turned into a cumulative deficit of $6 trillion."[17] On the eve of the global financial crisis and Great Recession, both of which led inevitably to a sharp decline in revenues and increased outlays, the country was ill-prepared to absorb their wrenching effects. America's running room to stimulate the economy by more tax cuts and more spending was constrained by the deep hole it was already in.[18]

We recount this history to shine a light on the misleading and factually incorrect rhetoric of amendment advocates like Mitt Romney and Mitch McConnell. Elected officials are not waifs amid forces. The president and Congress have in the past taken steps to restrain and eliminate deficits. In recent decades, the Democrats have been more attentive to the need to reduce deficits, while the Republicans have made tax cuts their highest priority. Government spending does not inexorably grow. Tax increases do not inevitably diminish economic growth, nor do tax cuts automatically promote it. Similarly, tax cuts do not force reductions in spending ("starving the beast" doesn't work), nor do tax increases foster spending increases.[19] The relationships among taxes, spending, deficits, and economic growth are highly contingent on a host of other factors. It would be foolhardy even to try to restrict or direct economic policy making with a balanced budget requirement in the Constitution. The message of the balanced budget amendment is, "Stop us before we spend or tax again." The system, when it was functional, showed that it can do that without changing the Constitution. The argument that government is so out of control that only a nuclear option of this sort will work is entirely bogus. The amendment would not end or reduce the dysfunction. It would diminish the Constitution and render the country less capable of effective self-governance.

Term Limits

The quintessential bromide for curing the ills of American democracy is to limit the number of terms anyone can serve in Congress and in state legislatures. Whenever public ratings of Congress drop from their normal bad to horrible or disastrous, count on someone to trot out this hardy perennial. And so it is again today.[20] The case is a familiar one: career politicians representing safe seats lose touch with their constituents, become beholden to the Washington establishment, feather their own nests, and fail to act in the broad public interest. Term limits would replace professional politicians with citizen legislators, whose brief time in office would maximize their incentives to act on behalf of their fellow citizens, inoculate them from the allures of lobbyists and other Washington elites bearing gifts, and restore Congress to its intended role as the citadel of deliberative democracy.

The last time term limits were all the rage was in the early 1990s, when the House bank and postal office "scandals" coincided with Newt Gingrich's aggressive push to end the near-permanent Democratic control of Congress. Conservative columnist George F. Will wrote a well-regarded book, *Restoration*, published in 1993, which provided the intellectual firepower for the term limits movement.[21] Advocates proposed initiatives in states where they were available to impose term limits on their legislatures, almost all of which the public approved.

Twenty-three states also adopted provisions that effectively limited the terms of U.S. senators and representatives in their respective state delegations. These state laws pertaining to Congress were declared unconstitutional by a 5–4 decision of the Supreme Court, which ruled that neither Congress nor the states could add such a qualification for serving in the House or Senate.[22] Only a constitutional amendment could impose term limits for members of Congress, though not for state legislatures. Candidates (mostly Republicans) ran for office pledging to support a constitutional amendment and to limit their service in office if such an amendment were not adopted and ratified. The amendment subsequently failed to garner the necessary two-thirds vote in the House, and some but by no means all of those members honored their pledge. The Supreme Court decision severely weakened the political force behind term limits for Congress, but the final nail in its coffin was the 1994 Republican landslide. Republicans had finally seized the reins of power in Congress, which led many term-limits supporters to lose their zeal. The limiting case was George Nethercutt of Spokane, Washington, who beat Speaker Tom Foley by calling him out of touch after too long in office, and made his six-year term limit pledge the centerpiece of his 1994 campaign—until he approached his third reelection campaign, when he reneged on that pledge. He was not alone.

This seems an unlikely time for term limits. Congress has just experienced three successive elections that brought many new faces to Washington and twice shifted party control. Populist Tea Party members fit almost perfectly the profile of citizen legislators that term-limit advocates favor and are making their presence felt. If anything, their determination to stick to their principles has reinforced partisan polarization in Congress and further weakened its deliberative capacity. What is most lacking in Congress today are members with institutional pride and loyalty, who understand the essential and difficult task of peacefully reconciling diverse interests through processes of negotiation and compromise.

George Will's embrace of term limits as a means of restoring deliberative democracy always struck us as bizarre. An admirer of the framers of the Constitution and of Edmund Burke, he is an odd champion of a centerpiece of the Anti-Federalists, who opposed the ratification of the Constitution and preferred to instruct and, if necessary, recall their representatives rather than have them exercise their own judgment in Congress. Theirs was a platform to weaken the republican features of the proposed new government, to keep the public's government on a tight leash by strengthening direct democratic controls. The Anti-Federalists lost the battle over the ratification of the Constitution, but they continue to be an animating force in American politics—in the Gingrich-led Republican Class of 1994 and most recently in the Tea Party–powered takeover of the House in 2010. So it is no surprise that limiting terms of legislators continues to reappear on the reform agenda.

Fortunately, we now have some actual experience of term limits with which to assess their likely effects. Between 1990 and 2000, twenty-one states adopted limits on the number of terms their legislators can serve (although six states ultimately overturned the limits).[23] Scholars have evaluated their effect on the legislators' responsiveness to their constituents, the expertise of legislators relative to others such as staff and lobbyists, and the power of the legislature relative to the executive.[24]

Ardent supporters of term limits cannot help but be disappointed by their findings. Term limits did not usher in a new era of citizen legislators. They neither altered the characteristics of those elected to office nor dissuaded them from pursuing other elected offices, building professional careers in politics, or becoming lobbyists. If anything, the limits amplified the corrosive effects of ambition on the legislators, who focused from day one on how best to use their limited time as a springboard to their next post. That produced incentives to go for a big, short-term splash and leave the long-term mess to the next wave of their successors. A legislator who spent less time in a legislative body acquired less specialized knowledge and relied more on others. Legislative party and committee leadership weakened, and legislatures lost ground to governors and their staffs. Term-limited legislators actually became less beholden to the constituents in their geographical districts and more attentive to other interests. And term-limited legislatures were less productive and less innovative in the policies they formulated.

Limiting terms of public office is, in our view, utterly unresponsive to any significant dimension of dysfunctional politics. It belongs in the same trash container as a smug reverence for the status quo, independent presidential candidates, and balanced budget amendments. Thanks, but no thanks.

Full Public Financing of Elections

Another response to the dysfunctional political system is the public financing of elections. As we discussed in Chapter 2, we take seriously the problems surrounding contemporary campaign finance law and practice and are greatly dismayed that the course Chief Justice John Roberts' Supreme Court has taken has effectively shredded the regulatory system and returned campaign finance to a state of nature. The opportunities for vast aggregations of individual and corporate wealth to influence the shape of governments and the policies they produce have multiplied.

The transparency of such donations and expenditures has sharply declined.[25] Fund-raising considerations dominate the normal routines of elected officials and political parties. The presence of so much interested money in campaigns contributes to the public loss of faith in the integrity of decision making. These and related problems associated with money in politics merit the attention and energy of advocates working to counter them; we include ourselves among this group.

But full public financing of elections is not the answer. We understand the appeal of the argument that eliminating private funding would reduce the power of special interests, powerfully made by Harvard Law professor Lawrence Lessig in his book, *Republic, Lost: How Money Corrupts Congress and a Plan to Stop It*.[26] His diagnosis of what ails America's representative democracy (not evil, but good souls corrupted) and his prescription for healing it (breaking the dependency on campaign funders) appear at first blush to be a strong antidote to dysfunctional politics. Lessig's signal achievement, nonetheless, provides an opportunity to explain why we believe too narrow a focus on money and politics is likely to prove unproductive.

Interest-group politics influence policy making in Congress, and the financial resources that interest groups bring to bear on the election of its members are a very important, but by no means only avenue of that special-interest influence. Economic interests like corporations, the Chamber of Commerce, community bankers, or labor unions can mobilize constituency support or opposition; hire former members, congressional staffers, and other seasoned operatives to gain access and deploy policy expertise within their lobbying operations; and invest heavily in shaping the broader policy community. Groups like the National Rifle Association and AARP can mobilize powerful collections of single-minded and passionate members and followers to point out the consequences to lawmakers if they don't heed the groups' message. Campaign donations and expenditures are a relatively small part of the resources they invest in government relations.

Moreover, governing is about much more than interests. Ideas and, especially in recent years, political ideologies matter. Indeed, the ideological polarization of the parties is at the center of dysfunctional politics and, as we argued earlier, this is not simply a phenomenon of political elites. Ideology motivates much of the money deployed in campaigns. Institutions matter as well. Money is not responsible for the mismatch between parliamentary-like political parties and the governing institutions in which they contest for power and policy. Reducing the role of filibusters in the Senate may be more productive than altering rules of campaign finance.

This brings us to the second point. Whether or not campaign money is the key to the influence dynamic in Washington, restricting the flow of private money in politics has proven devilishly difficult, and the actions of the Roberts Court and the feckless Federal Election Commission have made it virtually impossible. We are witnessing an explosion of so-called independent spending groups raising hundreds of millions of dollars from wealthy individuals and corporations that are in many respects appendages of a party or presidential candidate, or formed for the sole purpose of electing or defeating a particular congressional candidate. Candidates' direct financing of campaigns could well become a small part of the funding game in the near future. Incumbents will become ever more concerned about a potential spending effort that these groups might launch against them. They will be keen to keep their options open for raising large sums to counter that possibility.

Under these conditions, any reform effort that seeks to limit candidate fund-raising to small donations and public supplements seems quixotic at best. Full public financing of campaigns or the clean-money versions that have become the focus of recent reform efforts depend upon candidates voluntarily opting into a system that requires them to limit their fund-raising to small donations (usually set at a maximum of $100) plus public matching funds or $50 democracy vouchers that all registered voters may allocate to candidates as they wish. That increasingly looks like unilateral disarmament. Until there is a different majority on the Supreme Court or a constitutional amendment giving Congress the power to regulate donations and spending in federal election campaigns, more modest efforts to encourage small-donor fund-raising seem more in order.

The extreme and asymmetric partisan polarization that has evolved over several decades, initially reflecting increasing ideological differences but then extending well beyond issues that ordinarily divide the parties to advance strategic electoral interests, fits uneasily with a set of governing institutions that puts up substantial barriers to majority rule. To improve that fit—either by producing less polarized combatants or by making political institutions and practices more responsive to parliamentary-like parties—we as a people need to think about ambitious reforms of electoral rules and governing arrangements. But the more recent arrival of the Republican Party as an insurgent force in politics—one that has proven quite destructive to the process and substance of policy making in these troubled times—also requires our more immediate response. We need to identify ways of improving the performance of voters and politicians within the existing system, starting in the 2012 elections. The next three chapters will explore each of these remedies.

Fixing the Party System

I f the proposals we discussed in the last chapter are bromides to avoid, what then constitutes an affirmative agenda for improving the performance of America's dysfunctional politics? It starts with addressing the most problematic features of the party system, including the vast ideological gulf between the parties, their increasing internal homogeneity, the prevalence of constituencies safe for one party or the other, the news organizations and outside groups' reinforcement of ideological purity and extreme partisanship, and the rough parity between the parties nationally that contributes to the intensity and stakes of conflict. All these factors together produce a hotly contested, never-ending permanent campaign to control the White House and Congress. The asymmetric polarization that has recently developed has made the poisonous brew that these characteristics of the party system pose for governing within the U.S. constitutional system and political institutions even more toxic.

As we have described in earlier chapters, much of the dysfunctionality Americans observe in their government is a direct consequence of the GOP's unabashed ambition to reverse decades of economic and social policy by any means available.

Political parties play a crucial role in every well-functioning democracy. They organize a complex political world into digestible choices for voters and provide a basis on which elected officials can act for their constituents and the country and for which citizens can then hold them accountable. Party differences are essential to democratic choice and political accountability. We make no brief for weakening parties, delegating excessive authority to nonpartisan entities, or elevating bipartisanship as an inherently more constructive and responsible basis of policy making. Instead, we seek parties that are less ideologically polarized, more accepting of each other's legitimacy, and more open to genuine deliberation and bargaining on issues of fundamental importance to the future of the country. Most importantly, America needs parties that can function constructively in a governance system that requires an unusual degree of consensus to act.

While we can locate no single institutional fix, we have identified three avenues of electoral reform that have some promise of cooling the war between the parties. The first is to moderate politics by expanding the electorate. Higher turnout would pull more citizens with less-fixed partisan and ideological commitments into the electorate. Near-universal voting (achieved through Australian-style mandatory attendance at the polls, which we explain more fully later) would virtually eliminate the parties' incentive to diminish the turnout of those likely to support their opponent and to mobilize their strongest supporters.

The second is to reduce the presumed bias against moderate voters and candidates by altering how votes in the election are converted into seats in government. The most visible proposal is to reduce the gerrymandering of legislative districts that produces more lopsided constituencies for the two parties. Another is to replace closed primary elections, which attract ideologically skewed electorates that favor similarly disposed candidates, with open or semi-closed primaries. Finally, instant runoff voting (IRV), where voters can rank their candidate preferences, and electoral arrangements that provide a degree of proportional representation offer some promise of reducing polarization.

The third avenue of electoral reform seeks to break the polarizing dynamic of the parties through changes in campaign fundraising and spending rules and practices. The most promising methods are to mobilize large numbers of small donors and to enforce the transparency and genuine independence of super PACs and their nonprofit affiliates.

Expanding the Vote

A political system that restrains its citizens' voting is vulnerable to two corrosive phenomena: turnout in which the most motivated voters, usually ideological activists, have much greater leverage than their numbers would indicate, and a temptation by partisan political operatives to manipulate turnout to their own advantage, often by suppressing votes of those favoring the other side. Both phenomena have afflicted American democracy and contribute mightily to the polarization the country faces today and questions about the legitimacy of election outcomes. The process of manipulating voters and elections has led to a series of contested elections that have inflamed partisans and decreased public trust in the election process.

That reality suggests that Americans should explore multiple ways of making voting by eligible citizens easier, not harder, while guarding sufficiently against voter fraud and illegitimate manipulation of the voting process. They should also expand the vote to reflect more accurately the sentiments and orientations of the broader citizenry, not the smaller extremes. There are many avenues to consider.

Modernizing Voter Registration

Many of the problems with voting in the United States stem from a bulky and outmoded voter registration system in which the burden of registration is on the individual voter. In virtually every other established democracy, the burden is on the government. In the U.S., every state has its own system and requirements, and many lack the modern technology to ensure that they can track a highly mobile population of voters, who move frequently within cities and states and across state lines.

The Pew Center on the States has noted:

> In the 2008 general election, an estimated 2.2 million eligible Americans were unable to cast ballots due to problems with their voter registrations. Outdated and inaccurate voter rolls and a heavy dependence on new voter registrations submitted by unregulated third-party groups led to troubling questions about the integrity of our elections. To make matters worse, antiquated paper-based registration systems imposed unnecessary costs and administrative burdens on state and county election offices already facing severe fiscal constraints.[1]

What to do? First, the states should automate the registration system, so voters can register online and take their voter records with them when they move.[2] Automating registration—moving from paper to electronic records—is both cheaper and more effective. In South Dakota, registration at the Department of Motor Vehicles increased eightfold after the system was automated.[3] Nine states currently offer online registration (Arizona became the first, in 2002), with other states still awaiting implementation. The process is both easier for voters and dramatically less expensive for states and localities. Online registration for all Americans, which nonprofit groups such as the Pew Center on the States and the Brennan Center for Justice at NYU have recommended, should be a long-term goal.[4] It offers an additional advantage, because voters themselves are sending information directly to election officials; the potential for data entry errors diminishes, likely translating into more accurate voter rolls.

Second, local governments should harness the private sector to help create better, more reliable, and more up-to-date voter lists. The lists, which determine whether voters are qualified to vote, are essential to the system. There are many outside databases that can match with voter registration lists to verify records and keep lists up-to-date. Local governments responsible for building, maintaining, and updating voter registration lists can save money via such data sharing. The process can also reduce partisan manipulation of voter rolls by offering a range of objective databases to merge and purge voter lists; eligible voters being kept off the rolls either inadvertently or intentionally is less likely.

Third, computer technology could give voters more flexibility in where they vote, so a person who works long hours away from his local polling place would be able to vote more easily. Governments should allow hassle-reducing features such as an option to vote near work or at polling centers. Easily accessed and equipped sites like superstores and arenas would make it much easier for people to vote at convenient times. For several years, voters in Larimer County, Colorado, have been able to vote at Walmarts and other sites that have ample parking and are more convenient. The result? A systematic study comparing Larimer County with a county that lacks vote centers shows that the centers increased turnout by 2.5 percent to 7.1 percent.[5]

Fourth, nationally implemented election-day registration (EDR) would further spur increases in turnout. A number of states, including Wisconsin, Maine, and Minnesota, have implemented it. One nonpartisan report finds that voter turnout in states with EDR averages 10 to 12 percentage points higher than states without EDR.[6] States that are demographically and culturally disposed to higher turnout have been more likely to adopt EDR than other states. Nonetheless, the evidence demonstrates a significant, independent boost in turnout from EDR. Unfortunately, that positive impact has led to partisan (Republican) efforts in some states to roll back EDR, evidently out of concern that the increased turnout will benefit Democrats. Ohio and Maine passed laws ending EDR, but in Maine, where EDR has been widely popular, voters overwhelmingly rejected the repeal.[7] As with many of these reform ideas, sustained energy and resolve are needed to overcome both inertia and partisan opposition. The Maine example suggests that there will be sizable voter support for these ideas, which may grow as frustration with dysfunction leads more Americans to seek appropriate reforms.

Fighting Efforts to Restrict Voting

A larger problem in the era of dysfunction is that America also needs to vigorously fight the efforts to restrict and manipulate votes. Republican-dominated state governments in places like Kansas, Indiana, Georgia, and South Carolina, among others, have moved aggressively in the past two years to narrow the franchise for partisan political gain. These states have altered their voting rules, both by instituting tough voter ID laws and by using other ploys such as disenfranchising previously legitimate former felons, eliminating EDR, and reducing early voting in areas where Democrats have voted in advance of Election Day. Florida's Republican governor and legislature, for example, eliminated early voting on Sunday in an effort to thwart African-American churches' efforts to get out the vote.

Laws requiring voters to present photo identification at the polls should also make the IDs and any necessary documents, like Social Security cards and birth certificates, available for free. They can help those in poor neighborhoods where many residents cannot easily travel to government centers to obtain documents. But many Republican-dominated states are creating huge roadblocks to make it much harder for certain groups of Americans to get those IDs. The Associated Press reported on a study in South Carolina showing that African-American voters are disproportionately hurt by that state's new voter ID law.[8] In Texas, the political intent of its voter ID law is clear: voters can use a concealed-weapon permit to vote, but not a student ID. In New Hampshire, the Republican House speaker told a Tea Party gathering that he supported the law because it would decrease student voting: "They're foolish. Voting as a liberal, that's what kids do."[9]

Concerted efforts to raise roadblocks for voting haven't been evident since the days of the poll tax in the 1950s and 1960s— a move in Southern states that effectively disenfranchised poor black voters. And the efforts may increase: laws to restrict or constrain voting via voter ID or other methods in Mississippi, Texas, and South Carolina must currently be cleared in advance by the U.S. Justice Department under the Voting Rights Act of 1965.

But the Supreme Court has already come within an eyelash of striking down the preclearance provision of the Voting Rights Act (naturally, by a 5–4 vote). Congress should consider a new voting rights act to implement national protections for voters. The act would presumably go beyond the Southern states included in the original act and should have provisions like the following:

- Mandate that people must be able to obtain any IDs required for voting for free—including not just the IDs themselves, but costly supporting documents, like birth certificates; mandate that all voters would be able to find such IDs widely available at reasonably accessible sites, including mobile vans, if there are no offices within ten miles of eligible voters.

- Allow civil rights groups and the minority voters they represent to "opt in" to the Voting Rights Act by filing an administrative complaint with the Justice Department when their voting rights are constrained. Election reform expert Heather Gerken has suggested this approach as a way to protect minority voters while getting rid of the Roberts Court's likely argument for why Section 5, the preclearance provision, is unconstitutional.[10] This opt-in provision could cover the entire nation, without trying for the much harder expansion of the Voting Rights Act to all states.

- Require that polling places accept valid student IDs on equal terms with any government-issued ID.

- Mandate that any identification requirement contain a provision—as Rhode Island's voter ID law does—allowing voters who lack an approved ID to confirm their identity and have their votes counted, by signing an attestation that matches their signatures on file with their voter registration.

- Reward states that adopt best voting practices or enact policies that result in voter turnout gains generally, as well as specifically among minority, young, older, and disabled voters, perhaps with extra federal funds to administer elections or to buy voting machines.

- Create a separate federal ballot. The problems with disastrous election disputes such as the 2000 presidential contest and votes using the infamous and convoluted "butterfly ballot" in Palm Beach County, Florida, are often caused by election officials who cram too many local and state contests, along with ballot initiatives, on the same ballot with presidential and congressional elections. A separate federal ballot, using a nationally acceptable format, would have a maximum of three contests (president, Senate, House). It would eliminate costly sideshows such as the 2000 dispute or the one in a 2008 congressional race in Sarasota, Florida, caused by poor ballot placement for the House candidates. Such disputes add to the partisan division and high levels of voter distrust.

Moving Election Day

The organization "Why Tuesday?" which Norman Ornstein helped to form, has regularly asked prominent political figures, including presidential candidates, if they know why the United States votes on Tuesdays. Almost none have answered correctly, and many, including veteran lawmakers, mistakenly believe it is a constitutional provision. In fact, Tuesday voting stems from an 1845 law, enacted because of market day. In early agrarian American society, Saturday was for farming, Sunday was the Lord's day, Monday was for travel to the polling places at the county seat, Tuesday for voting and return home, Wednesday for market day, and Thursday for work.

In contemporary nonagrarian America, Tuesday voting is inconvenient for many working people; surveys show that 25 percent or more of nonvoters say that work or conflicting schedules impeded their ability to vote. For many people, the only opportunities to vote on Election Day are early in the morning, before work, or in the evening after work. The polls are usually the most crowded at these times, with long lines that discourage people. One solution is to pass a law that would change the federal Election Day to the weekend, as countries such as Iceland, Sweden, and New Zealand do (and some American states, like South Carolina, do for primaries); the best solution would be a twenty-four-hour election period from noon Saturday to noon Sunday. This schedule would eliminate Sabbath conflicts and give voters many more opportunities to get to the polls. If a weekend voting law were accompanied by a three-day early voting period on the Wednesday, Thursday, and Friday before the election, people away for the weekend would be able to vote at the polls as well.

Making Attendance at the Polls Mandatory

In both primaries and general elections in the United States, party professionals and consultants focus on bases: how to gin up the turnout of the party's ideological base and suppress the turnout of the other side. Nothing has forced discourse and political strategy away from the center to the extreme more than that focus. It has encouraged a concentration on hot-button issues that appeal to the party bases, like guns, abortion, immigration, and same-sex marriage, and led to more and more extreme rhetoric and exaggerated positions to accomplish the larger political goals.

Our earlier suggestions, if implemented, could significantly expand the electorate, but none would be as effective as adopting a version of the Australian system of mandatory voting. As the political scientist William Galston has noted, "Thirty-one countries have some form of mandatory voting, according to the International Institute for Democracy and Electoral Assistance. The list includes nine members of the Organization for Economic Cooperation and Development and two-thirds of the Latin American nations. More than half back up the legal requirement with an enforcement mechanism, while the rest are content to rely on the moral force of the law."[11] The Australian model would work best for the United States.[12]

In the Australian system, registered voters who do not show up at the polls have to either provide a reason for not voting or pay a modest fine, the equivalent of about $15. The fine increases with subsequent offenses. People do not *have* to vote. They can cast a ballot for "none of the above." Individuals can avoid the fine by providing a written excuse, such as for illness or travel. But the possibility of a fine has proven to be a powerful motivator, in the same way a five-cent tax on shopping bags in the District of Columbia has motivated people to bring their own bags or walk out of the supermarket juggling an armload of cans. In Australia, after over seven decades under the law, the result is a turnout rate of more than 95 percent, with roughly 3 percent choosing the "none of the above" option.[13] The fine, of course, is an incentive to vote, but the system has also instilled the idea that voting is a societal obligation.

Higher turnout is a desirable goal, but it does not necessarily mean a healthier democracy. Witness the "elections" in the former Soviet Union, which claimed a 99 percent turnout. The Australian system has also elevated the political dialogue. Australian politicians across the political spectrum have told us that it changes the way they campaign because they know that all their fellow citizens, including their own partisans, adversaries' partisans, and nonpartisans will be at the polls. The way to gain votes does not come from working the base to a fever pitch, but from persuading the centrists—the same kinds of voters who are increasingly left out of the American political process. In Australia, a candidate appealing to the extremes is destined for failure.

Ideally, the U.S. Congress would pass a law making poll attendance mandatory for federal primary and general elections. Of course, the chance such a law would pass is, in a favorite phrase of George W. Bush, "slim to none, and slim just left the building." Surveys show that substantial majorities of Americans oppose mandatory voting. Americans don't like compulsory anything; they value the freedom not to vote. But they may change their opinions after another lengthy period of dominance by political extremes and the divisive discourse, agenda, and outcomes that follow.

Mandatory voting comes with a price: a modest loss of freedom. But the revitalization of the rapidly vanishing center in American politics and the diminishment of the ideological base would more than balance that loss. If more Americans began to call for mandatory attendance and to educate others about why it would benefit the political system, it might become feasible as a long-term solution.

Another option is to provide an incentive rather than a disincentive. Mickey Edwards, a scholar and former Republican lawmaker from Oklahoma, suggested to us that the government offer voting Americans a $10 credit on their income tax bills (perhaps a refundable tax credit for poor people). The cost to the Treasury makes that option less than likely, but other possible incentives may have the same effect. One feasible option is a lottery—an election PowerBall with a large prize, in which a person gets a ticket in exchange for a voting receipt. Lottery mania could enhance turnout substantially. That said, we prefer a change that strengthens the civic fabric of society, one with responsibilities and opportunities for citizens.

Converting Votes into Seats

Another approach to encouraging less ideologically polarized parties is to diversify the constituencies of candidates seeking election or reelection to the Congress and state legislatures. Redistricting reform could reduce the number of seats that are overwhelmingly safe for one party or other; adopting primary rules that open up the process to give less advantage to the most ideologically extreme activists and voters; and using alternatives to the single-member district, plurality systems that are most common in U.S. legislative elections.

Redistricting Reform

The United States is an outlier in the democratic world in terms of how politicians shape the rules that affect their own electoral fortunes. This factor is especially notable in establishing legislative district boundaries. While most countries with single-member districts use nonpartisan boundary commissions to redraw lines so they reflect population shifts, in America most state legislatures create the maps for both congressional and state legislative districts through the regular legislative process. Gerrymandering— the manipulation of district boundaries to protect or harm the political interests of incumbents, parties, or other groups—began in the early years of the republic and has been a source of controversy and criticism throughout American history. Since the Supreme Court in the 1960s established the "one person, one vote" (equal population) requirement, each decennial census has set off a wild scramble across the country to garner political advantage while meeting the letter of the law. This picture is not pretty, and there are many good reasons for changing the redistricting process as some states already have, most recently, California.

For our purposes here, however, the question is whether such reform would make the parties less ideologically polarized and more willing to work together in a deliberative process. The answer is not as simple as it might first appear. The danger facing moderate candidates for office has metastasized to other levels like the Senate, where constituency lines never change and redistricting is absent. Redistricting would most likely not create widespread change. The U.S. Senate offers a prime example. Jiggered districts did not cost Republican Senator Robert Bennett of Utah even the chance to run for his party's renomination for his seat or unseat Lisa Murkowski in an Alaska Republican senatorial primary. Nor did they move then Senator Arlen Specter to switch parties in Pennsylvania, which he candidly admitted was because he simply could not win a Republican primary against an arch-conservative foe. Given the larger changes in partisan dynamics, imagining that a massive change would occur with redistricting reform would be foolish.

On the one hand, scholars have demonstrated that gerrymandering accounts for at most a modest share of the recent polarization.[14] To be sure, partisan and bipartisan gerrymandering in individual states has paid dividends in the form of seat gains for the party controlling the process or safe seats for incumbents of both parties. Egregious examples of politicians deciding who their voters will be (before voters have the opportunity to decide which politicians will represent them) are manifold. But a host of factors, including the geographical clustering of like-minded citizens and the inevitable trade-offs between partisan gains and safe seats constrains the national impact of such self-interested mapping on the number of lopsided Democratic and Republican districts. Removing all political manipulation from redistricting would very likely increase partisan fairness within states and marginally grow the number of competitive seats, but it is no panacea for the ideological polarization of the two parties' constituencies.

On the other hand, redistricting reform could play a very constructive role in curbing the extreme partisanship that extends well beyond ideological differences. Redistricting has become a major front in the permanent campaign of both parties. The parties devote enormous energy and resources to winning control of key state legislatures and governorships and then designing, enacting, and defending in the courts the maps that advance the interests of the controlling party. Party members in Congress and state legislatures find their own interests in reelection and majority status importantly connected to these efforts, which makes them even more inclined to cooperate with the strategic partisan team play that drains the policy-making process of its deliberative capacity. One needn't see gerrymandering as the major source of partisan polarization in order to believe that redistricting reform can contain and possibly reduce the escalating partisanship in American politics and ameliorate the poisonous ideologically driven culture.

The menu of possible reforms is familiar.[15] One reform is to delegate authority to an independent redistricting commission. Some states have chosen this option, most recently after citizens' groups utilized the initiative process. California, particularly notorious for noncompetitive congressional and state legislative districts, turned to an independent commission for its post-2010 redistricting. Its 2012 election results will show if that effort worked. The structure and rules of redistricting commissions shape their processes and outcomes; they can suffer from the same pathologies as the usual process if not designed properly.

Judicial intervention in the redistricting process has been common since the Supreme Court's landmark decisions in the 1960s, starting with *Baker v. Carr*. It might be a promising avenue for constraining gerrymandering. Based on provisions of the Voting Rights Act, federal courts have acted to prevent minority-vote dilution as well as to limit the extent to which states can take race into account in drawing boundaries. They have also enforced the equal population standard, although their exacting standard on one person, one vote to the exclusion of other considerations may well have facilitated rather than constrained gerrymandering. Virtually all redistricting maps are now subject to aggrieved parties' challenges in federal or state courts, but courts have little basis or inclination to step into the thicket of partisan gerrymandering.

Another approach to reform is to alter the redistricting standards that govern the process in individual states. Florida, a swing state in presidential elections that has overwhelming Republican majorities in its House delegation and state legislature, is drawing districts under new standards approved by a voter initiative designed partly to limit gerrymandering that protects parties and incumbents. Most state redistricting standards—

dealing with such matters as contiguity, compactness, adherence to existing political and geographical boundaries, and respect for communities of interest—have had relatively limited impact in constraining gerrymandering. Some states are addressing this by adopting explicit standards for partisan fairness, competition, and politically blind redistricting.

Another fruitful approach is to increase transparency and citizen involvement in the redistricting process. Some states have adopted requirements to hold public hearings, post all data used by redistricting authorities as well as draft maps on public websites, and provide ways that citizens can submit alternative maps. Reformers have come up with a number of initiatives, including one in which we have helped, to develop mapping software and make it widely available. By using the open-source software available at www.publicmapping.org, anyone can draw district lines with real census data and maximize criteria such as communities of interest (cities, counties, even neighborhoods), partisan competitiveness, or geographic compactness. Then anyone can contrast the results with the highly manipulative plans of political actors and consultants and make them available to courts if the political plans fail.[16] Use of the public mapping software in Virginia and Michigan showed that it is indeed possible to create districts equal in population but much better in representing natural communities of interest and fostering electoral competition. Much work remains to be done to empower this form of citizen involvement.

Changing to Open Primaries

In virtually all contests for the Senate, House, governorship, or state legislature, candidates must win their party primary before moving to the general election. Thus, party election laws are crucial, but they vary greatly among the states.[17] So-called closed primaries limit participation to voters who declare their party affiliation at a specified time before the election. Semi-closed primaries allow independents to participate and/or allow new voters to register and choose their party on the day of the primary. Open primaries come in two forms: (1) Blanket primaries feature a single ballot with candidates from all parties; all participants may vote office by office in some or all of the party primaries. The top vote receiver from each party becomes that party's nominee in the general election. (2) Top-two vote-getter (TTVG) primaries are formally nonpartisan. Candidates may list a party preference but not a party affiliation. All voters choose office by office from among all candidates. The top-two vote receivers (even if both list the same party preference) face a runoff in the general election.[18]

Not surprisingly, closed primaries tend to produce lower turnout, attract more ideologically extreme voters, and select fewer moderate candidates. Semi-closed primaries produce somewhat higher turnout, attract more ideologically diverse voters, and choose more moderate candidates. The differences between these two primary systems are modest but significant.[19]

Several states, including Louisiana, Alaska, Washington, and California, have experimented with open primaries. In 2000, the Supreme Court found California's blanket primary to be an unconstitutional violation of the parties' right of association. That prompted the state of Washington to replace its blanket primary with a TTVG system, which the Supreme Court subsequently upheld. In 2010, California voters approved an initiative establishing the same TTVG system, which is now in place for the 2012 election.

The form of open primary matters in terms of its ability to encourage a broad group of nonextreme voters to play a role in selecting candidates. TTVG proponents argue that their system makes it easier for relatively moderate candidates to be nominated and elected to public office. Empirical evidence of the impact of this form of open primary is very limited. The Public Policy Institute of California, which has carefully parsed the available evidence, concludes that TTVG is unlikely to change California's political landscape overnight and its overall effect will probably be modest.[20] This is partly because voters often cross party lines to support incumbents. Nonetheless, TTVG offers the possibility of producing more moderate elected officials after a period of adjustment. An added practical virtue of the open primary is that states can implement it more easily than reforms like mandatory attendance at the polls.

The objective of primary reform is to increase the number of moderate voters and candidates participating in the nomination process. While the outcome is uncertain, the likely direction of change surely merits states' further experimentation along these lines.

Establishing Alternatives to Winner-Take-All

The U.S. electoral system is dominated by winner-take-all rules. Single-member districts with plurality winners create powerful forces favoring a two-party system and an electoral geography producing vast areas of one-party dominance. This pattern was described many years ago as Duverger's Law, for French social scientist Maurice Duverger.[21] Many voters have little opportunity to elect a representative whose public views are consistent with their own. Third-party and independent candidates have virtually no chance of winning elections; at best, they can aspire to be spoilers by drawing enough votes from the most broadly preferred candidate to produce a plurality victory for the major-party opponent.

Even presidential elections, which are inherently winner-take-all (only one president at a time), are problematic. When all the electoral votes in each of forty-eight states are allocated to the plurality winner of the popular vote in that state, it creates the possibility and occasional reality of mischief—the election of a candidate who loses the national popular vote or whose victory results from the presence of an independent or third-party spoiler.

The states could deal with some of these drawbacks by using the above-mentioned Australian-style instant runoff voting (IRV), sometimes called the alternative vote.[22] Voters rank candidates in order of choice, allowing ballot counts of a single round of voting to perform like a series of runoff elections. Until a candidate receives a majority of votes, ballots cast for the lowest-placing candidate are redistributed according to each voter's next choice. IRV produces majority winners, eliminates the spoiler role, and reduces the "wasted vote" calculation for minor-party candidates, allowing them to participate more fully in the election process and work to build their party's support. IRV would also complement a presidential election system based on a direct national popular vote. Building more legitimate majorities in this fashion (by eliminating the Electoral College and plurality outcomes) could well extend the electoral reach of the major parties and thereby reduce their ideological polarization.

A more ambitious way of pushing this same logic is through proportional representation (PR). Based on the principle that any group of like-minded voters should win legislative seats in proportion to its share of the popular vote, PR facilitates the direct representation of racial and political groups and encourages multiparty systems and broad coalitions within legislatures. There are many types of PR systems, but the one that the United States might be most able to adapt is the single transferable vote

(STV) with multimember districts, that is, more than a single candidate is elected at large from the same constituency.[23] To be elected, candidates need not capture a majority, just the share of the vote determined by the size of the electorate divided by the number of positions to fill. Each voter gets one vote, which can transfer to another candidate in accordance with that voter's instructions if his or her first choice already has enough votes or has no chance to be elected.

The United States has had some modest experience with multimember districts in state legislative elections, and the results are encouraging. Illinois, for example, has experimented successfully with such a system. There is no constitutional impediment to using multimember districts in congressional or state legislative elections, although a federal law passed in 1967 requires single-member districts for elections to the House of Representatives. The historical experience in the U.S. with alternative electoral systems and the more wide-ranging comparative evidence across the democratic world suggest that some form of PR would reduce the impact of gerrymandering, increase turnout, better represent minority interests, provide a more accurate representation of majority popular sentiment, and encourage depolarization in the current party system.

We are in no way full-throated adherents of moving fully to proportional representation; some PR systems in Europe and elsewhere encourage a splintering of the party system, with extreme parties arising because they can get a foothold and seats in the legislature and force unnatural coalitions in which extreme groups hold the balance of power. In Israel, where the threshold for representation is particularly low, ultrareligious parties have in effect held coalition governments of the left, center, and right hostage for decades to extreme policies that do not reflect the positions or desires of the country's majority. We recognize that the details of any such plan are important, the complications and trade-offs significant, and the uncertainty far from trivial. But it would be shortsighted to ignore the costs of winner-take-all electoral politics and refuse at least to consider viable alternatives.

Funding Campaigns

The path to significant restrictions on an out-of-control money system after *Citizens United* is steeply uphill. The Federal Election Commission, which has three Republican commissioners determined to nullify federal election law, would need dramatic change—something President Obama could achieve, at the cost of infuriating Senate Republican Leader Mitch McConnell, by aggressive use of his recess appointment power. And the five members of the Supreme Court who made up the majority in *Citizens United*—justices Kennedy, Roberts, Alito, Scalia, and Thomas—would also need to change. What can reformers do?[24]

First and foremost, reformers must aggressively try to restore the effectiveness of two provisions of the law the Court affirmed in *Citizens United*—(1) disclosure, and (2) the separation of independent expenditure groups from the candidates and campaigns they support. One legislative remedy, the DISCLOSE Act, passed the House in the 111th Congress but as we noted earlier, died in the Senate on a filibuster by a single vote. As another tragic example of asymmetric polarization, every single Republican, including all those who had strongly supported campaign finance reform like Olympia Snowe of Maine and John McCain, voted against it.

The DISCLOSE Act would have required the organizations running independent spending campaigns to disclose the identity of their large donors and to reveal the donors' identities in any political ads they fund. (To avoid opposition from the nonprofit community, the bill exempted all long-standing, nonprofit organizations with more than 500,000 members from having to disclose their donor lists.) A stripped-down bill would be a useful antidote to the poisonous interaction between huge money spent on campaign ads and subterfuges to ensure the contributors can remain anonymous. For all the reasons we suggest in Chapter 2, unlimited contributions are themselves deeply corrupting, but disclosure at least provides some form of prevention.

Inadequate disclosure is not the only problematic feature of super PACs that needs attention. Another is the fiction that their so-called independent spending activities are truly free of the candidates and parties they support. The requirement of independence is routinely honored in the breach by nearly everybody participating in the super PAC farce. Two court decisions in 2010—*Citizens United* and *SpeechNow* (the latter a decision of the Court of Appeals for the District of Columbia)—allowed unlimited contributions to independent expenditure-only PACs. But the Federal Election Commission's "advisory opinions" laid out rules for the so-called super PACs and gave them a green light for mendacity that makes laughable the candidates' claims that they have no connections with the super PACs created in their names.

To start, Congress could pass a new law sharply tightening the anti-coordination provisions that require unlimited donations to be totally independent of candidates and their campaigns. Every serious presidential candidate has a super PAC that can collect unlimited amounts for "independent" expenditures; people who are intimates of the candidates, often directly from their campaigns, run those "independent" groups. The idea that they do not communicate with or coordinate with the candidates and their campaign operatives defies common sense. A Rick Perry campaign ad in late 2011 used extensive video footage taken directly from Perry super PAC ads. Another FEC loophole allows the *candidates themselves* to appear at super PAC fund-raisers, so long as they do not directly solicit unregulated money. The super PACs are plainly an avenue for candidates to evade the law that limits contributions. A PAC created for the purpose of supporting a single candidate is itself a violation of the law requiring independence, but the FEC has refused to implement regulations that would make that clear and ban such behavior.

Even the political parties have now formed their own super PACs, albeit through legally independent organizations but staffed by former party officials working aggressively to advance partisan interests in the election. These groups reinforce and exacerbate the partisan divide, and do so in a way that mocks the notion of independent spending. Super PACs are starting to form to boost individual members of the Senate and House.

A new law that flatly outlaws the super PACs would be the best route. But as the DISCLOSE Act vote in the 111th Congress shows, passing any campaign reform law without sixty Democrats in the Senate and a Democratic majority in the House is next to impossible. Also close to impossible would be reform of the FEC or a new set of commissioners, at least as long as Mitch McConnell remains Senate Republican Leader; he has made it clear that protecting the FEC as it now exists, that is, as a lawless agency, is a top priority for him. As Public Citizen's Craig Holman has noted, "[McConnell] is really the whole key to the FEC. . . . He realized several years ago that a very effective way to minimize the effect of federal laws is to undermine the regulator."[25] So absent a recess appointment strategy on the part of the president, the government has to look for other options to provide disclosure and prevent brazen and illegal coordination. As a first option, the Justice Department could prosecute violations of the coordination bans in cases where the brazen behavior has been most evident. Justice does not need to wait for the FEC.

Other federal agencies could take the same route. Consider the problem of 501(c)4s: their designation under the Internal Revenue code enables a nonprofit social welfare organization, which must operate primarily to further the common good and general welfare of the people, to engage in lobbying and advocate for issues. As we outlined in Chapter 2, operatives like Karl Rove and Norm Coleman have manipulated the IRS process to create 501(c)4s that are parallel to their other organizations—either directly political ones (called 527s) or think tanks—so that they can raise unlimited sums for campaign purposes from undisclosed individuals, corporations, or unions.

The way the Rove and Coleman organizations have operated, using their 501(c)4s for election-driven activities clearly designed as their fundamental and overwhelming purpose, is a direct distortion of the intent of the law and the IRS regulations. It is possible to file an application with the IRS to create a 501(c)4 and operate as one for a year before the IRS rules on the application. In the meantime, the organization can raise and spend millions of undisclosed and unlimited contributions and flood them into ads to affect elections, and not have to file a tax return until long after.

To stop this behavior, the IRS would have to enforce its own regulations, not because one party or the president demands it, but because it is the agency's duty to see that its regulations apply as intended. The IRS started in 2011 with a tentative plan to require the donors to the faux-501(c)4s to pay a gift tax on their donations, but it drew back after criticism from conservatives, both political operatives like Karl Rove and media figures like

Rush Limbaugh, who like the lack of disclosure. The IRS should go further and entirely deny the designation to organizations misusing the 501(c)4 status and fine those who do so.

Another avenue of reform is through the Federal Communications Commission. As former FCC Chairman Newton Minow and former FCC General Counsel Henry Geller have pointed out, "Section 317 of the 1934 Communications Act provides that viewers and listeners are entitled to know who is paying for commercials. This is true of advertising not only for commercial products, but especially in the case of elections or controversial issues."[26]

To implement the law, the FCC has long stipulated that television and radio stations disclose the identities of those who pay for the ads. Minow and Geller continue, "The longstanding FCC regulation requires an announcement to 'fully and fairly disclose the true identity of the person or persons . . . or other entity by whom or on whose behalf such payment is made.' It provides that when a person or entity acts on behalf of another, and this fact is known or could be known by the station exercising reasonable diligence, the name of the real sponsor must be announced."[27]

The FCC has begun regulatory action to require stations to electronically compile information on their public interest obligations and to put it online for viewers or others to examine. Going the next step—requiring the stations to disclose in real time the identities of all significant donors who paid for political ads and to acquire the information from the ad buyers—is clearly within the agency's purview and would create the appropriate disclosure that the Court has applauded and the FEC has blocked.

The Securities and Exchange Commission could require all public corporations to disclose in their annual or quarterly reports the monies they have spent for political contributions or issue advertising, including monies paid to third parties, like the Chamber of Commerce, that now are hidden from public view. Of course, this step would not affect private corporations, but would be a giant move forward from the current situation.

The executive branch could also have some effect here. In 2011, the White House drafted an executive order to require all private contractors who do business with the federal government to disclose their spending on political activities. These contractors already have to disclose their direct contributions to candidates and parties; this order would only extend current regulations to the new forms of political activity via so-called independent groups that are clearly designed to influence the outcome of elections. Implementing the executive order would be an appropriate way to extend disclosure. All it needs is presidential approval.

Finally, corporate and investor rights groups could target corporations' political spending practices to establish accountability for their decisions to allocate resources for political campaigns and to require full disclosure of all such spending to the board of directors, shareholders, and the general public. The Center for Political Accountability has begun that effort, with some initial success.[28]

Reforming Leadership PACs

Disclosure and tightened rules governing coordination are not the only ways to ameliorate the broken campaign finance system. One area in serious need of reform is so-called leadership PACs, created and run by individual lawmakers using the same rules as other regular PACs, which have been growing in number and reach since the mid-1990s. In FEC parlance, these are called "unconnected" PACs. Opensecrets.org describes them this way:

> Politicians collect money for their own campaigns—we all know that. But many of them also raise a separate pot of money, commonly called a leadership political action committee, to help other politicians. By making donations to members of their party, ambitious lawmakers can use their leadership PACs to gain clout among their colleagues and boost their bids for leadership posts or committee chairmanships. Politicians also use leadership PACs to lay the groundwork for their own campaigns for higher office. And some use their PACs to hire additional staff—sometimes even their family members—and to travel around the country or eat in some of Washington's finest restaurants. The limits on how a politician can spend leadership PAC money are not especially strict. Also, lacking a requirement that lawmakers disclose their affiliations with leadership PACs, these committees have been able to slip under the radar for years.[29]

Opensecrets.org tallied 265 such PACs, with well over $9 million in contributions for the 2012 election cycle before the end of calendar year 2011. The development and expansion of leadership PACs, in which congressional figures, including all the top party and committee leaders, use their clout with donors to raise money and then distribute it to their colleagues or candidates, all to advance their own political careers, add to the corrupting influence of money inside Washington. Lawmakers rise to positions of committee and party leadership not based on their talents or expertise but on their prowess at shaking down big money donors. The more active role of party leaders in raising money for their "teams" adds to the sharp divisions of the permanent campaign. Leadership PACs should be eliminated.

Prohibiting Lobbyists' Contributions

Odd as it may seem to cite Jack Abramoff as a character witness about the evils of political money—a bit like citing the Marquis de Sade on the evils of torture—he may be the best eyewitness to the deeply corrosive and corrupting effect of the money culture. Abramoff believes that anyone who has or seeks a contract with the federal government or is trying directly to influence governmental decisions should be prohibited from making campaign contributions. In his book, *Capitol Punishment: The Hard Truth About Washington Corruption From America's Most Notorious Lobbyist*, Abramoff suggests reforms include banning donations from lobbyists and those who receive public funds:

> Instead of limiting the size of every American's political contribution, we need to entirely eliminate any contribution by those lobbying the government, participating in a federal contract, or otherwise financially benefiting from public funds. If you get money or perks from elected officials—be "you" a company, a union, an association, a law firm, or an individual—you shouldn't be permitted to give them so much as one dollar. It does no good to ban Jack Abramoff from giving $2,000 to Congressman Badenov, but allow the members of his law firm to pick up the slack. If you choose to lobby, if you choose to take money from our nation, if you choose to perform federal contracts, or if you draw your compensation from any entity which does, you need to abstain from giving campaign contributions. It's your choice either way. But you have to choose one, not both.[30]

A law banning certain American citizens from contributing to campaigns will quickly run afoul of the First Amendment. But a congressional rule that says lawmakers may not accept a contribution for themselves or for their parties from anyone lobbying Congress or participating in a federal contract is another matter. Admittedly, this is unlikely to happen. But it is a goal for lawmakers.

The Next Generation of Reform

Discussing next-generation campaign finance reform when *Citizens United* and its progeny remain as the driving forces behind political campaigns may seem fruitless at best. Once unlimited money becomes the rule and the wall between independent efforts and candidates breaks down, any serious efforts to alter the fundamentals of the system, short of a constitutional amendment, are like erecting a thin line of sandbags to alter the course of a tsunami.

But pursuing a new framework for campaign finance remains a key component for reducing dysfunction in the American polity. One reason is history: for ideas in this realm to reach fruition or be enacted takes years or decades. A second reason is that even a thin line of sandbags is better than none. A third is that a new framework—one based more on incentives than restrictions—has the potential to take the issue of reform out of the courts, where it is ill suited for balanced and reasonable resolution, and into the political sphere.

In 2010, we joined with Michael Malbin of the Campaign Finance Institute and Anthony Corrado of Colby College to create a new working group on campaign finance reform. The four of us had worked together more than a decade earlier coming up with a set of ideas that helped shape what ultimately became the

Bipartisan Campaign Reform Act. This time, we wanted a model that took into account not just the Supreme Court decisions and the regulatory environment but the vast technological changes that had altered communications, including social networking, and also the nature of political fund-raising because of the ubiquity of the web and web purchases.

The 2008 Obama campaign demonstrated that it is both possible and cost-effective in the Internet age to raise a lot of money from many small donors. Just a few years earlier, the only effective way to have a massive number of small donors was through the use of direct mail, an extraordinarily costly tool; some 95 cents of every dollar raised had to be poured back into the costs of creating and maintaining mailing lists and sending out letters to solicit donors. Using the Internet cut those costs to a handful of pennies on the dollar. And raising the money also enabled Obama to engage and involve a wide range of donors throughout the campaign and created a robust and ongoing social network of supporters.

Our working group recognized that taking full advantage of the communications revolution required universal access to affordable high-speed broadband and full access by all carriers for political speech. We strongly supported the creation of a one-stop portal for a citizen to access all election-related public information.

But the core of our report, called "Reform in an Age of Networked Campaigns," was a strong endorsement to redefine public funding of campaigns through a multiple matching fund for small donors in primary and general election campaigns for candidates who receive more than a reasonable threshold of such contributions; to abolish spending limits as a condition for public funding; to require candidates who accept the matching funds of public dollars to abide not by any spending limit but by lower but reasonable contribution limits; to provide "seed money" by offering early money sooner to newly emerging candidates; and to encourage small donors by offering tax credits or rebates for their contributions.[31]

A system built around a four-to-one or five-to-one match for small donors would give candidates a powerful incentive to spend more time finding a large number of small donors and less time trolling for the larger ones. Expanding the number of people giving even small amounts to a campaign would mean more engaged citizens. And a system that also would enable parties to have unlimited coordinated spending for their candidates if the money were all raised from small donors creates a more realistic and better campaign dynamic.

This kind of reform is no panacea for the oceans of unlimited money now flooding the system, but it is the best way to provide at least some countervailing force.

Many of the reforms we discuss in this chapter would require a long time and a lot of discussion to enact; others have only a tiny chance of implementation. But as voter disgust with dysfunctional politics grows in intensity, the market for ideas like public financing or even mandatory attendance at the polls will also grow.

Reforming U.S. Political Institutions

W e are tempted to think big when it comes to reforming political institutions, because the problems are so large and so vexing. But wholesale change in the political system is not possible and might not work. So in this chapter, we will focus on smaller ways to change American institutions to better fit the contemporary parties and political culture.

The boldest way of dealing with the mismatch between the party system and governing arrangements would be to make the governing institutions and processes fully compatible with parliamentary-style parties. The current presidential system, based on the independent election of the president and Congress, features a strong separation of powers with checks and balances. If this system were replaced with a parliamentary one in which a parliamentary majority (one party alone or in coalition with others) elects the executive, it would ensure substantial cooperation in the formulation and enactment of the government's program. The mismatch would evaporate.

The debate on the relative advantages and disadvantages of parliamentary and presidential systems is a fascinating one.[1] But a country understandably proud of the world's oldest constitution and long accustomed to an independently elected president is unlikely to take it seriously. The root-and-branch restructuring of the Constitution that would be required to establish a parliamentary democracy makes any such consideration purely academic.

Short of such a major constitutional restructuring, the system could eliminate the midterm elections that regularly diminish the strength of the president's party in Congress, often leading to divided-party rule. Although divided government has not been a huge obstacle to policy making throughout much of the country's history, it has become downright destructive in this era of polarized parties. If members of Congress ran for election only in conjunction with presidential elections, the incidence of divided-party government would be reduced and presidents would have a more realistic time frame in which to put policies in place and be held accountable for their consequences. But this change too would require a constitutional amendment: altering the length of terms to four years in the House and four or eight years in the Senate.

Beyond the difficulty of enacting such a constitutional amendment, moving to elections every four years instead of every two would require a wrenching transition for Americans accustomed to regularly holding elected officials accountable at the polls. There could also be significant unintended consequences. Increasing Senate terms to eight years would mean a lengthy time without reelection; reducing Senate terms to four years, while at the same time increasing House terms to four years, would alter fundamentally the nature of the Senate as a distinct body.

Our tack here is to consider institutional changes consistent with the current constitutional framework that would improve the fit between our current parliamentary-style parties and the policy-making process. The first change is to strengthen majority rule in the Senate. As we highlighted earlier, winning control at both ends of Pennsylvania Avenue is no guarantee that the president and his majority in Congress can move decisively to staff the administration and deliver on campaign promises.

The minority party in the Senate has an effective veto over a president and his majority party. Senators' overuse of the filibuster has created a routine supermajority hurdle that the framers never anticipated and that has not occurred before in American history. No other democratically elected leader around the world faces such a hurdle. Eliminating or reducing the scope of Senate actions subject to filibuster-related obstruction would allow the majority to resolve highly contested issues and to conduct Senate business in a timely and electorally responsive fashion. Changes in Senate rules to make both filibusters and holds less burdensome and vexing would make a huge difference when the president enjoys majorities in both congressional chambers.

A second way of improving the fit between the parties and governing arrangements is to shift decision-making power between Congress and the executive branch. It might entail more aggressive unilateral use of executive power; follow the model of the Federal Reserve or various independent regulatory agencies by removing some public decisions from the orbit of the president and Congress; or make more extensive and powerful use of nonpartisan, expert panels such as the Independent Payment Advisory Board authorized by the Affordable Care Act. A shift in power from Congress to the executive branch has been a striking feature of American government with the rise of the administrative and national security state, but Congress has retained substantial law-making and oversight resources. Further transfers of authority might improve the fit of the governing institutions with the contemporary party system but drain Congress of its comparative advantages in the constitutional system of checks and balances. But some modest shifts to give more leeway to the executive make sense, given the current and continuing dysfunction.

Restoring Majority Rule in the Senate

As the December 2011 Senate recess approached, Republicans again used the filibuster and other delay tactics to block confirmation of more than fifty presidential nominations for the State, Defense, and Justice departments, along with the new Consumer Financial Protection Bureau housed at the Federal Reserve and several posts at the Environmental Protection Agency. Among them was the Public Printer of the United States, a wholly uncontroversial appointment that both parties endorsed. Senate Republican Leader Mitch McConnell threatened to hold up even more nominations if President Obama considered using his constitutional recess appointment authority to circumvent any of the filibusters. McConnell did allow votes on several ambassadorial nominations before the Senate left for the holidays, but this was after many had been twisting in the wind for months. Others failed to get the sixty votes needed for cloture, even though all had majority support.

There are several principles that can and should apply to the Senate and its filibuster rules and procedures. First, the Senate rules should allow only one filibuster on any bill, where now there can be two or more. In the Senate, there is a motion to bring a bill to the floor for consideration and then debate on the bill, including amendments and a substitute. There can be other debates on creating and approving conference reports after the bill has passed. Each stage for a single piece of legislation is currently subject to a separate filibuster. Second, if a filibuster is applied, the minority party should have the burden of taking the floor and holding it via debate; the majority party should not have to keep the Senate in session by providing the quorum. Third, the Senate rules should eliminate extraneous delays outside the filibuster itself. And fourth, the Senate rules should guarantee a vote on executive and judicial nominations reported out of committees, with a time limit for holds on the nominations. Several senators, including Mark Udall of Colorado, Tom Udall of New Mexico, and Jeff Merkley of Oregon, have recommended specific reforms. Mark Udall's reform package is particularly balanced and realistic.[2] We believe the reforms should include the following elements, based on some of the best ideas proposed by various senators.

Limit Filibusters to One per Bill

Currently, a senator can apply filibusters separately to the motion to proceed to the bill, on a substitute, on the bill itself, and on the three motions required to get the Senate to conference. As we documented in Chapter 3, many bills that passed unanimously were first stuck with two filibusters, each requiring days and days to quash, taking up more floor time for no good reason. Once a supermajority has made clear that it wants to end debate and move to vote, that should be it. The Senate rules should eliminate all those filibusters except for the one on the bill itself. That means the majority leader has the authority to bring any measure to the floor without a motion to proceed.

Put the Burden on the Minority, Not the Majority

In the Senate rules, a cloture motion to end debate and move to a vote takes three-fifths of the Senate. Thus, the burden is on the majority to provide sixty votes, if all one hundred Senate seats are filled, to stop a minority from blocking action. During the 111th Congress, in Obama's first two years, Democrats were forced on at least one occasion to bring the ailing, ninety-one-year-old Senator Robert Byrd out of his hospital bed to cast that sixtieth vote. That seems perverse to us. (Byrd, a stickler for Senate rules but also a believer in Senate civility, cried out "Shame!" to the Republicans in the body from the floor.) If the idea behind a filibuster is that a minority feels so intensely about an issue that it puts everything on the line to prevent action, then the minority should go the extra mile to prevail, not the majority that wants to act.

The burden is on the majority in another way. In the past, a filibuster meant that the majority would stop all other action in the Senate and debate the filibustered issue twenty-four hours a day to dramatize the stakes behind the filibuster and to enable the minority to show its mettle and demonstrate why it was taking this extreme action. In the 1950s and 1960s, Southern Democratic senators filibustering civil rights bills wanted to take the Senate floor and debate nonstop around the clock for days to highlight their emotional, vehement opposition.

More recently, filibusterers have had no interest in actually . . . filibustering. Their goal has been to obstruct quietly, without facing any blame for disrupting the Senate or Americans' lives. The rules now make it easy for them just to lift a baby finger, declare their intention to filibuster, and raise the bar to sixty senators without any strain. How? By simply withholding their agreement to a unanimous consent request, the obstructionists put the majority into a box; keeping the Senate in session to dramatize the cost of obstruction requires a quorum of fifty-one senators. Without a quorum, there is no session and no ability to highlight and showcase the obstruction going on. If the Senate cannot get the quorum, it cannot meet, which is fine with the filibusterers. So to keep the Senate going, the majority must supply a quorum around the clock, giving its members cots to sleep on while the Senate drones on. If the minority keeps one member on the floor who can object to any unanimous consent agreement and to note regularly the absence of a quorum, it can get its way while its members can sleep at home or work outside the Capitol grounds.

This problem arose inadvertently when the Senate reformed its filibuster rule in 1975, changing a cloture requirement of two-thirds of senators present and voting to a requirement of three-fifths of the entire Senate. That reform seemed to lower the bar for cloture, but actually complicated it by forcing the majority to continually provide sixty votes. If the reformed standard were a proportion of those present and voting, then the majority, if it had a quorum of fifty and there were only a few minority members on the floor, could prevail on a cloture vote with as few as thirty members (three-fifths of the fifty senators making up a quorum).

One simple reform to correct that problem and force the minority to keep its members in or near the chamber when it conducts a full-fledged filibuster would be to change the cloture bar to three-fifths of those present and voting. A better and stronger reform would be to require forty-one votes to continue the debate, not sixty votes to end the debate, putting the burden squarely on the minority where it belongs.

Eliminate Extraneous Delays

If a senator threatens a filibuster, a cloture motion to block it and move to a vote has to "ripen" for two days. When a cloture motion succeeds, Senate rules provide for thirty hours of debate after cloture. The "debate" is not a debate at all, just thirty hours of precious Senate floor time with no need for anyone to take the floor to discuss anything. Two simple changes are in order: First, reduce the two-day delay in a cloture motion to one day. Second, divide the thirty hours of debate into fifteen hours each for the majority and the minority. Allow the majority to waive its fifteen hours, and require the minority to actually debate on the floor for its fifteen hours.

Minority senators insist that the reason they call for so many filibusters is that the Majority Leader, who uses a device called "filling the amendment tree," shuts them out of the process of amending bills. The Majority Leader can use his or her power of recognition, that is, the power the leader has under Senate rules to supersede all other senators and gain the floor, call up a bill, and offer enough amendments and amendments to amendments to preclude any other alternatives, hence, the "amendment tree." The minority members have a point. In return for streamlining the process, finding a way to allow a minority alternative on most bills, without filibustering, is a reasonable trade-off. One solution is to have a nondebatable motion to allow the minority a single, germane amendment by a simple majority vote, even after the Majority Leader has filled the amendment tree to preclude minority amendments.

Expedite the Nomination Process

Senators Charles Schumer, Lamar Alexander, Susan Collins, and Joseph Lieberman raised reformers' hopes in 2011 when they proposed reducing the number of Senate-confirmable executive positions by over two hundred and streamlining the forms required of nominees. These forms are time consuming, cumbersome, and costly for the nominees, both delaying their confirmations and impeding their willingness to be considered for appointments.

But their efforts, as the McConnell action in December 2011 demonstrates, have done nothing to alter the nomination process. And that process is thoroughly broken. Beyond the use of filibusters, we have had the expanded exercise of individual holds to kill nominations, not simply delay them for a period of time. Senate rules should allow guaranteed up-or-down votes on the floor on all executive nominees within sixty days after being reported out by the committee of jurisdiction. Sixty days is ample time for senators to muster their arguments to reject nominations, and also provides reasonable time for nominees who can win confirmation to take office without disruptive delays. The other filibuster reforms we recommend will be enough to expedite action on judicial nominations, which as lifetime appointments should have a different threshold than executive ones.

Achieving such ambitious reforms of filibuster-related Senate rules faces three daunting obstacles. The first is the provision in the current rules that requires a two-thirds majority to cut off debate on a rule change. This provision was a part of the 1975 reform compromise to lower the cloture threshold to sixty senators. The second is each party's fear of being steamrollered by the other when it finds itself in the minority. The third is the perception among senators of both parties that their ability to place holds on nominations and legislation, which is derived from the filibuster, is a major source of their individual power in the Senate.

We believe that the Senate, like the House, is reconstituted after each election, in spite of the fact that only a third of its members is elected every two years. As such, according to common law understanding of democratically elected legislatures and the presumption of the Constitution, a majority of its members have the right to set its rules for each Congress.[3] This so-called "constitutional option" is highly controversial, and exercising it would upend decades of precedent in the Senate. But we believe it is entirely legitimate; senators could use it, if only as a threat, to compel both parties to acknowledge that their institution has fallen into utter disrepute and dysfunction and that a major change in the rules is essential to restoring its place in American democracy.

Senators' acknowledgment of dysfunction, accompanied by increasing public scrutiny of its current rules and practices, might help overcome the partisan and individual interests that have frustrated past reforms.

Shifting Authority Between and Within the Branches

Allowing majorities in the Senate to prevail more often would be the most direct way of making the branches of government more compatible with polarized parties. But its effectiveness would dramatically diminish in periods of divided government because the president's party would lack even a simple majority. Another approach, particularly attractive to presidents dealing with one or both chambers of Congress controlled by the other party, is to transfer more decision-making power from Congress to the executive branch. Such shifts between branches have occurred throughout American history, mostly from the legislature to the executive, but occasionally featuring congressional efforts to reclaim authority unabashedly asserted by the president.

This changing balance between the branches is an inevitable consequence of a constitutional system that enables separate institutions to compete for the exercise of shared powers. But the struggle between the president and Congress to control domestic administrative and regulatory processes and to exercise authority over a wide range of national security matters has intensified with the increasing polarization of the parties. The Reagan administration's effort to advance its conservative agenda throughout what it considered to be a politically hostile bureaucracy gained support from a theory of the unitary executive.[4] That theory holds that the president, as the single head of the executive branch and constitutionally charged to "take Care that the laws be faithfully executed," has broad authority to direct how executive branch employees perform their duties, and that Congress's authority to check presidential actions is extremely limited.[5] A stronger version of the theory legitimized a very aggressive and controversial assertion of the president's unique and unchallengeable authority during the George W. Bush administration, particularly given seemingly permanent threats to national security after the terrorist attacks of September 11, 2001.[6]

Recent Democratic presidents have shown no affinity for the unitary executive theory, with good reason. While most scholars, the two of us included, believe that the theory is way outside the bounds of the Constitution and the framers' intent, these presidents have not been reticent in claiming executive authority to take consequential, unilateral actions. In the face of strong opposition in Congress or an unwillingness or inability to resolve differences, presidents are naturally disposed to get done what they can on their own. President Clinton moved ambitiously to conserve public lands, protect Americans' medical privacy, and create a welfare-to-work partnership. After the devastating

Democratic defeat in the 2010 midterm elections, President Obama received many diverse recommendations for advancing a progressive agenda through executive actions.[7] He has moved forward on a number of these fronts. A recent example: in reaction to the inability of Congress to reauthorize the No Child Left Behind Act, despite bipartisan support and the leadership of Education Secretary Arne Duncan, the Obama administration liberally interpreted its authority to grant waivers to states in order to reshape federal education policy.

Whether shifts in policy-making authority between and within the branches compensate constructively for the pathologies of polarized politics is a matter of contention, with positions often determined by which party or ideological perspective gains an advantage with a particular change. Even the Federal Reserve— easily the most important and successful delegation of authority by Congress—routinely elicits sharp criticism and (unsuccessful) efforts by individual members of Congress to alter or reclaim parts of its authority. That criticism became heightened in the 2012 campaign with the prominence of unrelenting Fed critic and Republican presidential candidate Ron Paul, and the embrace of his criticism by fellow candidate Newt Gingrich. But with a statute that keeps its funding and operations beyond the reach of normal congressional and presidential controls, the Fed steers monetary policy without harmful political interference. Paul and Gingrich notwithstanding, independent central banks with exclusive jurisdiction over monetary policy are widely considered essential components of modern economies. It is hard to imagine another area of public policy in which Congress would be willing to grant this degree of autonomy.

Congress has established independent regulatory agencies with an eye toward limiting the direct authority of the president.

Most agencies (though not all) are headed by multimember boards or commissions such as the Federal Communications Commission, Federal Trade Commission, or Securities and Exchange Commission, whose members are appointed to fixed, staggered terms by the president and confirmed by the Senate. A president may appoint no more than a bare majority from his own party and may not remove members without cause. These agencies typically have administrative independence, such as submitting their budgets and legislative proposals directly to Congress without Office of Management and Budget approval and litigating in court independent of the Justice Department.

Presidents can influence but not control the agencies' actions. (The same cannot be said of regulatory agencies embedded in executive departments. In a very controversial though entirely legal action, Health and Human Services Secretary Kathleen Sebelius decided in late 2011 to block the Plan B One-Step contraceptive pill from being sold to adolescents without a prescription. For the first time in American history, a cabinet secretary overruled a Food and Drug Administration drug-approval decision.[8]) Congress, on the other hand, retains substantial levers for control over independent agencies—confirming members, writing and revising statutory authority, approving budgets, and overseeing operations. Independence from the president serves as protection from political meddling in critical policy decisions that depend on a scrupulous review of scientific evidence. But it is less suited to adapting policy-making institutions to parliamentary-like parties.

Another form of organizational innovation is designed to overcome political obstacles when Congress is enacting necessary but controversial policy changes. The most frequently cited innovation is the Defense Base Closure and Realignment Commission

(BRAC). It was designed to overcome the Defense Department's political difficulty in garnering congressional approval for its recommended closures of outdated military installations that cost jobs to a member's constituents. While Congress as a whole agreed on the need for reductions and realignments of bases (along with the budgetary savings), individual members naturally opposed those slated for closure in their own districts or states. They had a powerful electoral incentive to use every means to keep them open. BRAC set up a process whereby it presents Congress a list of facilities to be closed; Congress then has forty-five days to approve a joint resolution of disapproval to prevent implementation. The list begins with the Defense Department's recommendations and is adopted with deletions and additions by a nine-member independent panel appointed by the president. Then, if the president accepts it in its entirety, it goes into effect unless rejected by Congress. Between 1988 and 2005, all five rounds of BRAC proposals produced major reductions and realignments of military installations.[9]

Many analysts have urged that BRAC be used as a model for dealing with budget deficits and debt. We earlier discussed Congress's rejection of a bill to establish a bipartisan commission along these lines, after seven Republican senators who previously cosponsored the bill voted to sustain a filibuster against it. President Obama responded by appointing a similar commission by executive order, but it lacked the guarantee of a timely up-or-down vote in the House and Senate. The Simpson-Bowles Commission was unable to reach the supermajority called for in its rules for approval of a deficit-reduction package, although its co-chairs issued a report with the support of a majority of its commissioners. The report attracted much attention and the favor of many budget experts, but it was never put into legislative form and submitted as a bill for Congress to consider. The twelve-member super-committee created as part of the deal that ended the debt ceiling battle was guaranteed a timely, up-or-down vote on its recommendations. But no procedural fix could overcome the gulf between the parties on reducing the deficit, and it failed to reach majority agreement on a package of budgetary changes. That failure meant a set of smaller automatic sequestrations scheduled to take effect at the beginning of 2013.

This recent experience confirms our view that a BRAC-like mechanism is not well suited for resolving deep differences on the broad issues of taxes and spending, particularly with the Republicans so deeply dug in—substantively and politically—to their position on tax increases. But it might be possible to utilize similar mechanisms on more focused and limited problems to achieve what is widely acknowledged as necessary, but not through the regular policy-making process. This option is represented by the Independent Payment Advisory Board, which was established in 2010 as part of the Affordable Care Act and charged with the mission of holding Medicare spending within legislative limits. Like BRAC, the IPAB was created because Congress was incapable of standing up to health provider and senior lobbies whenever it confronted reforms to cut costs in the Medicare program. Once fully implemented, the board is to recommend to the president ways of reducing annual per capita spending on Medicare pegged to specific targets. The president in turn is required to transmit those recommendations to Congress for consideration under expedited procedures. If Congress fails to approve them or alternatives that achieve comparable savings, the board's recommendations take effect and the Secretary of Health and Human Services must implement them.

The board faces major challenges—first to survive and then to function effectively.[10] It faces a Republican Party determined to repeal, disable, or weaken the entire health-care law of which it is a part. Critics allege that the board would impose price controls, create "death panels," and supplant congressional prerogatives. On the other side, statutes circumscribe the actual changes that it may recommend. The board's recommendations may not "ration" health care; raise revenues, premiums, or cost sharing; limit benefits or change eligibility standards; or reduce payments to acute-care or long-term-care hospitals or to hospices before 2020 or payments to clinical labs before 2016. These limits are serious constraints.

If the Independent Payment Advisory Board survives, if it receives adequate resources to carry out its responsibilities, and if it is strengthened statutorily, it could establish a potentially powerful portfolio of cost-control instruments within Medicare and other public and private health-delivery and financing systems, thereby doing more to confront long-term deficit and debt problems than any other reforms under consideration. But those "ifs" are highly problematic in this polarized political environment. The institutional changes needed to cope with America's serious governing problems face powerful resistance from the same political forces that exacerbate its difficulties in trying to govern effectively.

Navigating the Current System

We've looked at ways to take the urgently needed (if challenging) steps to bring the American party system and its governance institutions into better alignment. We've noted though that changing electoral rules and institutional arrangements will be at least as difficult as governing effectively is. We conclude by exploring how Americans can improve the political system they have.

Can Americans do anything in the near term without making massive changes in electoral rules and political institutions? First, they can work to change the culture that shapes how political institutions perform. Then they can confront directly the destructive asymmetry between the parties and demonstrate that voters have the capacity and bear the ultimate responsibility for healing a broken and very dysfunctional political system.

Changing the Political Culture

Trashing others, undermining their very legitimacy, and lying openly and repeatedly about individuals or institutions now bring no visible penalty or public obloquy. In fact, it can mean fame and fortune. Changing the country's poisonous culture, which has metastasized beyond the political area, requires first an effort to restore some semblance of public shame.

Restore Public Shame

The country needs the remaining (if dwindling) opinion leaders from institutions like the military, churches, universities, foundations, business, the media, and public life to outspokenly denounce those who profit from bombast and lies and to denounce equally the television and radio networks and the print outlets that give them airtime and web and print space, with the legitimacy that flows from them. There's no better place to start than with the outrageous rhetoric of Stephen Schwarzman, billionaire chairman of the Blackstone Group, who responded to a proposal from the Obama administration to treat the "carried interest" of private equity managers as ordinary income, taxable at a rate of 35 percent, instead of the same as capital gains and dividends, at 15 percent. Schwarzman characterized the proposal as being "like when Hitler invaded Poland in 1939."[1] Scores of such examples litter the landscape. In another particularly egregious example, the Speaker of the Kansas House of Representatives, Republican Mike O'Neal, referred to First Lady Michelle Obama as "Mrs. YoMama" and called her the Grinch, and then forwarded widely an e-mail that asked for Psalm 109 to be applied to the president—a verse which says "Let his days be few in number" and "May his children be orphaned and his wife a widow."[2] Then there was

Republican Representative Allen West of Florida who told President Obama to "get the hell out of the United States of America" in a January 2012 speech captured on videotape. People like Colin Powell, Robert Gates, Bill Clinton, Bill Gates, Tom Brokaw, George Shultz, and Oprah Winfrey, ideally through some collective effort, should have the goal of recreating in society some sense of shame for distortions, lies, and other efforts to coarsen the culture and discourse. That means calling out miscreants like Schwarzman, O'Neal, and West.

Tech companies like Google, Facebook, Apple, and Microsoft can also help by convening experts to explore ways of rooting out insidious and false communications spread over the Internet. They should do more than a onetime debunking via factcheck.org or politifact.org, but maintain a continuous and aggressive effort to spread the word when falsehoods (like the libel about Congress in the widely circulated e-mail discussed earlier or the birther nonsense) continue to spread or fade when debunked and then reemerge for a new generation or population to be misled.

Re-create a Public Square

America also needs a concerted effort to ameliorate the impact of the partisan media. The country no longer has a public square where most Americans shared a common set of facts used to debate policy options with vigor, but with a basic acceptance of the legitimacy of others' views. Little can be done to change the new business models, driven by technology and global economics, that make Fox News's approach a clear winner over the old network news approach. But a semblance of a new public square, one that might never have the reach or audience of the old one, could be a model for civil discourse and intelligent, lively debate.

The best way to create a public square is to find a new source of funding for public media, with shows like the *PBS NewsHour*, *Charlie Rose*, and the *Diane Rehm Show* that fit a better model of discourse. A strong option would be to change the model of broadcasting and the public interest that has been the law since 1934, one in which broadcasters can use valuable public airwaves for free, in return only for their paying heed to the public interest through amorphous public interest obligations.

Television broadcasters, the biggest beneficiaries of the post–*Citizens United* campaign finance laws, have covered less and less politics and government at all levels, even as their revenues from campaign ads have skyrocketed. Broadcasters have claimed that they give back in a single year more than $10 billion in public interest obligations. We propose erasing those obligations and instead requiring broadcasters to pay annual rental fees for their use of public airwaves amounting to a quarter of the burden they themselves say they incur. This $2.5 billion each year could go to a public or private foundation that would create more opportunities for candidate-centered discourse during campaigns; for genuine, straightforward coverage of news and public affairs; and for more real debates on important issues. These efforts would not realistically compete with cable news outlets or commercial talk radio, but could attract a robust enough audience to provide a positive role model and a partial counterweight for more-corrosive media figures. The foundation could fund many more outlets than traditional public television and public radio, including new sources for information and discourse on the web and via social networking.

Create a Shadow Congress
We do not shrink from partisanship, but from tribalism. We recognize that not all policy differences in America divide sharply

along partisan lines. But two recent debates show how far the country has strayed. In the debate over health reform, some ideas that had originally come from Republicans and conservatives were trashed simply because Obama and Democrats had embraced them. In the debate over climate change, Republicans who sought bipartisan approaches, like former Representative Bob Inglis of South Carolina, were drummed out of office by their own partisans because they dared to acknowledge the problem and work with the other side.

Neither do we shrink from lively and contentious debate. But too often in the past few years, debates have moved from contentious to vicious, with challenges not so much to the workability or desirability of ideas as to the basic legitimacy of the ideas and their progenitors or supporters. The so-called "death panel" discussion and the trashing of the scientific community over climate change underscore that point.

What to do? In our conversations with former lawmakers from both parties, we are struck by their amazement, anger, and exasperation with their former colleagues; it is as if, once they left the peculiar air breathed inside the congressional chamber and inhaled a less noxious set of fumes, they were freed from a trance. We have thus thought of creating a parallel or shadow Congress of former lawmakers from across the political spectrum who would periodically gather and debate key issues facing the country.

Our goal would be to have the kind of debate and deliberation that Congress should engage in but, to be frank, rarely did even in better days. The best debate in Congress in many decades was conducted over American entry into the first Gulf War in 1991. It was stirring, emotional, consequential, and educational, but in both the House and Senate, it was more a series of sequential speeches than genuine give-and-take. There have been a few recent instances of genuine debate, in colloquies on the Senate floor over the National Defense Authorization Act, for example.[3] But they are rare.

A shadow Congress could expand those colloquies to a wide number of former lawmakers and encourage real give-and-take with heated exchanges, not all along strictly partisan lines. We would expect the members selected to appreciate the viewpoints of opposing colleagues and accept their legitimacy. Given the disrepute of the current, real Congress, the parallel Congress might well receive significant public attention, with its debates triggering additional discussions on public affairs shows like *Nightline*, *Meet the Press*, and *PBS NewsHour*, and perhaps encouraging local versions of the debates on individual public television stations. The debates could prove enlightening to viewers and listeners and might also provide a powerful role model for the real Congress to change its own culture of argument.

Reining in an Insurgent Outlier

In our long history of writing and commenting about American politics and Congress, we have criticized one or both political parties when it was warranted. We have noted, for example, that Democrats' arrogance and condescension toward the minority over their forty years of majority reign contributed in no small measure to the Republican takeover of the House in 1994, and we criticized the Democrats for their departures from the regular order during their renewed majority status after 2006. We also chastised Democrats when they used over-the-top rhetoric in the battle over Robert Bork's confirmation to the Supreme Court, and used the filibuster to block qualified nominees, including

Miguel Estrada to the Court of Appeals. So we do not in this instance level our criticisms at the Republican Party lightly, or as a partisan weapon.

In every chapter of this book, we have documented the ways in which the Republican Party has become the insurgent outlier in American politics and as such contributes disproportionately to its dysfunction.[4] If the case we have made about the GOP is accurate, then the culture and ideological center of the Republican Party itself, at the congressional, presidential, and, in many cases, state and local levels, must change if U.S. democracy is to regain its health. The contemporary GOP, to the horror of many of its longtime stalwarts and leaders like former senators John Danforth of Missouri and Alan Simpson of Wyoming, has veered toward tolerance of extreme ideological beliefs and policies and embrace of cynical and destructive means to advance political ends over problem solving. These tendencies have led to disdain for negotiation and compromise unless forced into them and rejection of the legitimacy of its partisan opposition (as manifested especially in the continuing drumbeat questioning the birthplace of President Obama, and the refusal of major party figures to condemn the birthers).

Some readers may be struck by a lack of balance in our treatment of the two major political parties. We hope they understand that we do not seek to advance a personal ideological or partisan agenda. Rather, we believe that imbalance or asymmetry reflects a regrettable reality that is too often obscured in the traditional media and among serious scholars of American democracy. We want two vibrant and constructive political parties that can compete vigorously for the votes of Americans and fight hard for their views in political and policy arenas. But the Republican Party of old—the party of moderates like Ray LaHood, David Durenberger, and John Danforth and of conservatives like Alan Simpson, Mickey Edwards, and Bob Bennett—is no longer present in our political debates or governing dynamic.

It is, of course, awkward and uncomfortable, even seemingly unprofessional, to attribute a disproportionate share of the blame for dysfunctional politics to one party or the other. Reporters and editors seek safe ground by giving equal time to opposing groups and arguments and crafting news stories that convey an impression that the two sides are equally implicated.[5] Scholars often operate at a level of analytic generality and normative neutrality that leads most treatments of partisan polarization to avoid any discussion of party asymmetry.[6] Many self-styled nonpartisan and bipartisan groups seeking to advance policy and process reforms are heavily invested in a search for common ground between the parties, a strategy made difficult if not untenable when one is a clear outlier.

We believe that our case for asymmetric partisan polarization is strong and that it has enormous consequences for the country's ability to deal with the existential challenges that confront it. Democrats are hardly blameless and have their own extreme wing and their own predilection to hardball politics. But as we have shown, those tendencies have not generally veered outside the normal boundaries of robust politics. At the same time, Republicans in office have driven both the widening of the ideological gap between the parties and the strategic hyperpartisanship on such crucial issues as financial stabilization, economic recovery, deficits and debt, health-care reform, and climate change. In the presidential campaign and in Congress, their leaders have embraced fanciful policies on taxes and spending and kowtowed to the most strident voices within their party. Where both parties in the past would try to focus debates on policy differences while using rigorous analyses from places like the old Office of Technology Assessment, the National Academy of Sciences, and the CBO, Republicans in the new era have dismissed nonpartisan analyses and conclusions about the nature of problems and impact of policies when they don't fit their own ideology or policy prescriptions. In the face of the deepest economic downturn since the Great Depression, the party leaders and their outside acolytes insisted on a one-sided obeisance to a supply-side view of economic growth while ignoring demand-side considerations. On issues from health reform to climate change to energy production, Republicans in Congress opposed, obstructed and tried to nullify policies proposed by President Obama that many of them had recently embraced, and repeatedly took hostages and made non-negotiable demands in lieu of real give-and-take. The Republican presidential debates and the rhetoric and positions of all the GOP presidential candidates have provided no basis for people to believe they would govern differently if they were to capture the White House and both houses of Congress.

How can the thoughtful and problem-solving element of the party that we have long admired, represented by such former lawmakers as the late Barber Conable of New York, Bill Frenzel of Minnesota, John Porter of Illinois, Tom Davis of Virginia, Nancy Kassebaum of Ohio, Howard Baker of Tennessee, and many others, be restored to return the party to its pragmatic conservative roots? How does this relate specifically to the choices voters will confront in 2012 and beyond?

Change from Within

Refreshingly (at least modestly so), not just disillusioned former elected officials and members of the conservative movement like economist Bruce Bartlett, but also a few of its most respected inside commentators, including the *National Review*'s Ramesh Ponnuru and the American Enterprise Institute's Steven F. Hayward, have challenged the destructive, take-no-prisoners approach of the movement within the Republican Party.

Ponnuru offered Republicans a gimlet-eyed view of their own electoral failings in 2006 and 2008 in a Bloomberg.com commentary. He notes:

> The view that Republicans must avoid accommodation at all costs—that the principal obstacle to achieving conservative policy goals is a lack of spine, and not, say, a lack of popular support—made them lose at least two Senate races in 2010. In Colorado and Nevada, conservative primary voters rejected two electable, conventionally conservative candidates because they were considered part of a compromising establishment. . . . Meanwhile, the real mistakes of the Bush years keep being made. Republicans had nothing to say about wage stagnation then and are saying nothing about it now. The real cost of Republicans' fixation on ideological purity is that it distracts them from their real problems, and the nation's.[7]

In a long, provocative, and thoughtful essay in *Breakthrough Journal*, Hayward makes a strong pitch for modernizing conservatism without diluting its strong philosophy.[8] He notes that the "no tax increase" mania of the movement, and its corollary, the theory that the way to reduce the size and scope of government is to "starve the beast," has been proven empirically not to work. Indeed, he quotes the seminal work of libertarian William Niskanen, who found that lower taxes actually increase the size of government, and that raising taxes may be the most effective way of reducing government by making voters pay for what they receive, instead of getting things at a steep discount.

Hayward further urges conservatives to recognize the reality that "the welfare state, or entitlement state, is here to stay. It is a central feature of modernity itself." Most importantly, Hayward takes on frontally the current destructive politics: "Achieving policy compromise and the reconstruction of a 'vital center' requires an end to the view of practical politics as a zero sum game, in which compromise is viewed as a defeat by both sides."

Hayward not surprisingly says both sides are responsible for the dysfunction and calls for both liberals and conservatives to reform themselves. His points about the weaknesses and failures of the liberal movement are well taken. But his willingness to defy convention and look inwardly at the failings of the contemporary conservative movement is a small but hopeful sign that over time, some changes might come from within.

The Power of the Citizenry

The most powerful potential leverage in any democracy is the ability of the citizenry to "throw the bums out." Scholars have demonstrated that voters often treat elections as referendums on the performance of the party of government (which they almost always associate with the president's party).[9] But this instrument of democratic accountability is especially blunt in times of polarized politics. It gives the opposition party a powerful incentive to obstruct the president's agenda and to discredit those elements that are adopted by turning their debate and passage into divisive and bitter wars. During periods of economic crisis, the opposition loses its incentive to alleviate Americans' pain and instead is encouraged to err on the side of allowing harmful conditions to fester as a price worth paying for political gain. The

Republicans responded to this latter incentive in a powerful and unprecedented fashion when they were in the minority during the first two years of the Obama administration. That strategy intensified in the third year, after Republicans won a majority in the House. Mitch McConnell's infamous quote left no doubt about their priorities: "The single most important thing we want to achieve is for President Obama to be a one-term president."[10]

Referendum voting in times of economic difficulty also tends to obscure the policy choices that the competing parties offer. One of the tenets of democratic theory is that the electorate will punish parties that become ideologically extreme—that stray from the preferences of the median voter. Yet so-called swing voters, pure independents or very weakly attached partisans, have little in the way of ideological frameworks or information on the policy positions of the candidates and parties with which to mete out that punishment. They are the classic referendum voters who simply bet that times will improve with different leaders. This phenomenon is by no means limited to the United States. Political scientist Larry Bartels has demonstrated that governing parties of all ideological stripes—right, center, left—were punished by voters during the economic crises of 2008–2011 while the ideological makeup of successful opposition parties was equally diverse.[11]

There is a final constraint on voters providing a way out of dysfunctional politics. Understandably, during difficult times such as the present, they tend to broadly condemn Washington or Congress, which is more likely to reinforce the structural dynamics that produce gridlock than to generate a constructive call to action. Voters simply turning out of power those now in control of the White House, Senate, and House or indiscriminately replacing incumbents with "outsiders" because of broken politics have little hope of making the parties and institutions operate more constructively and effectively. Instead, they are likely to have the opposite effect, and continue a downward spiral into deeper dysfunction.

Voters are unlikely to be more responsive to the problems they themselves identify without additional information about the policy and process choices that competing parties and candidates offer. But we have little confidence that a public consumed with pressing matters close to home will brush up on their civics and become fully informed citizens. America's is a republican (that is, representative) form of government, not a direct democracy. Political leaders and parties have the responsibility to structure and elucidate those choices. Along with the media, they are responsible for providing regular reporting and analysis that clarifies the substance of the choices and the likely consequences. But, ultimately, the public will reap what it sows.

Presidential Leadership and Campaign Strategy

President Obama came to office having promised the country postpartisan politics, built on the commonalities among Americans, not the divisive differences. Then reality hit. Obama's promise did not start with the 2008 campaign; it was the core of his famous keynote address at the 2004 Democratic National Convention, which established a political brand that facilitated his extraordinarily rapid ascent to the White House. But almost since his presidency began, allies and observers have criticized that outlook for pursuing bipartisan agreements in the absence of a sincere negotiating partner. A postpartisan approach to governing seemed simply naïve and wishful thinking, poorly suited to the sharply polarized system Obama confronted; this became crystal clear when Republicans announced their intention to operate as a parliamentary-like, unified opposition party.

Of course, some of the criticism was overdone and misplaced, at least for Obama's first two, quite productive years in office. He began his term when Democrats were short of the sixty votes needed for cloture in the Senate, so some Republican support was essential. Getting the House and Senate Democrats to agree on anything was difficult, while getting all Senate Democrats, from socialist Bernie Sanders of Vermont to conservative Ben Nelson of Nebraska, to unite was especially daunting. That took time and patience, including attempts at compromise with Republicans long after it became clear that they would not be cooperating. The modus operandi was a necessary step to assuage more conservative Democrats like Nelson, Blanche Lincoln of Arkansas, and Mary Landrieu of Louisiana that he was leaving no stone unturned in his efforts to find bipartisanship. That avenue was essential to get the remarkable unity from all sixty Democrats, in the brief period when they had the sixtieth vote, to pass the health reform bill.

However necessary that approach then, conditions clearly changed with the 2010 midterm elections and the advent of divided government, with the take-no-prisoners approach of the House Republican majority. Those conditions dictated that the president adopt a more confrontational, clarifying approach to Congress and the public. The debacle of the debt limit faux negotiations may have been necessary to make Obama recognize the wisdom of such an adjustment in his leadership strategy, but he clearly did so. And paradoxically, the more aggressive "tit-for-tat" strategy on his part, raising the political heat and stakes for those pursuing obstruction, may be the only way out of this prisoner's dilemma.[12] If carried through the last year of his term and integrated fully into the campaign, his strategy increases the prospect of making the election more a choice than a referendum.

As the ideological outlier, Republicans have every incentive to blur policy differences between the candidates and parties by focusing the public's attention on the performance of the economy under Obama's leadership. The Republican presidential nominating process made more publicly salient the stark rightward tilt of the GOP. Their objective in the general election campaign is to downplay those positions and frame the election as a referendum on Obama.

They also appear to be taking a calculated gamble: that even if voters become more enraged by Washington's policy failures and take some of their anger out on Republicans, they will still, thanks to the firewalls they have erected through redistricting to shore up vulnerable freshmen, be able to maintain a narrow majority in the House. At the same time, with only ten Republican seats at risk in the Senate compared to twenty-three Democratic seats, they can count on voter anger toward incumbents to give them the net gain of three seats to recapture the Senate. Unfortunately, that calculated gamble means a continuing willingness to block significant policy action if it might accrue to the benefit of Obama, even if the blockage results in more pain and dislocation for Americans.

Here, President Obama's belated willingness to call out Republicans specifically for obstruction has changed the dynamic somewhat, creating at least some political pain and potential political downside to Republican obstinacy. That in turn has meant some modest willingness on the part of Mitch McConnell to craft compromises with Harry Reid and President Obama when he believed that the downside risk of refusal to do so was too great.

What the Media Should Do

We have discussed the profound impact of the new media on American politics and governance and suggested how to contain its destructive effects and encourage the positive contributions that new technologies offer. Here we tender some unsolicited advice to friends and colleagues in traditional news organizations, where enormously talented individuals report, write, and broadcast under strong codes of professional conduct. Discerning consumers of their output—and we include ourselves—profit every day from their enterprise and insights.

That said, there is more they could do to help citizens navigate the current political system. Here are a few suggestions:

- Help your readers, listeners, and viewers recognize and understand asymmetric polarization. The parties are different in many important respects (which we have tried to identify in these pages). Document those differences, report on them, and consider the implications of those differences for ordinary citizens.

- A balanced treatment of an unbalanced phenomenon is a distortion of reality and a disservice to your consumers. A prominent *Washington Post* reporter sanctimoniously told us that the *Post* is dedicated to presenting both sides of the story. In our view, the *Post* and other important media should report the truth. Both sides in politics are no more necessarily equally responsible than a hit-and-run driver and a victim; reporters don't treat them as equivalent, and neither should they reflexively treat the parties that way. Our advice: don't seek professional safety through the unfiltered presentation of opposing views. What's the real story? Who's telling the truth?

Who is taking hostages at what risks and to what ends?

- Fact checks are important contributions to contemporary journalism. Why treat them all as equally important and bury them in the back pages? Move them into the body of news stories and onto the lead, and repeat them when politicians continue to repeat falsities despite the fact check.

- Stop lending legitimacy to Senate filibusters by treating a sixty-vote hurdle as routine. The framers certainly didn't intend that. Your consumers should be better informed of the costs associated with it. Report individual senators' abusive use of holds and clearly identify every time a minority party uses a filibuster to kill a bill or nomination with majority support. Do not say or write that Congress or the Senate killed a bill or stopped a nomination if a majority in both houses voted for the bill or the individual—say or write the truth, that the bill or person was blocked *despite* majority support, by the use of a filibuster. This is especially true, as with the example of the DISCLOSE Act on campaign finance, when all the members of one party (in that case, fifty-nine) support a bill and all the members of the minority vote against. It was not Congress that blocked disclosure—it was one political party via the filibuster.

- Your highest priority should be to clarify the choices voters face and the likely consequences of those choices after the election. How would they govern? What could they accomplish? What differences can people expect from a unified Republican or Democratic government or one divided between the parties? The "how would they govern?" story is always important, but more so now than ever.

The Voters Decide

Political elites can clarify choices, and the media can help make those choices understandable, but in the end, voters decide elections. Visceral disgust and blanket condemnation of Washington or Congress or government are often ill-informed and unproductive reactions; for politicians and their consultants, that can easily serve their self-interest and the status quo. Understanding the forces driving dysfunctional politics is essential to changing it, over the long haul, through reforms of the electoral and governing institutions, and sooner, through voters' strategic choices. We end with some suggestions for voters:

- Punish a party for ideological extremism by voting against it. (Today, that means the GOP.) It is a surefire way to bring the party back into the political mainstream.

- Promote the essential norms of the republican form of government (respect for opposing views, acceptance of the opposition party's legitimacy, bargaining, and compromise) by demanding that elected representatives and their parties adhere to the norms and punishing those who don't. When candidates pop up and proudly proclaim that they have nothing to do with politics or Washington, and won't behave like the politicians, ask them their views on those essential norms—and keep in mind that many, perhaps most, of the ardent and vocal outsider candidates reject them at their core.

- Consider carefully which presidential ticket (the candidates, party, and platform) you prefer to lead the country. Then entrust that party with the majority in the House and Senate. It makes more sense than divided government in these times of partisan polarization. But remember that actions have consequences, and votes based on either reflexively throwing the bums out, or spurning one's own party or president for insufficient zealousness, could bring in something far worse.

- Challenge the legitimacy of Senate filibusters and holds. The framers of the Constitution had no such devices in mind. A vocal backlash against obstructionism by the minority will do much to overcome gridlock and permit those in government to work more effectively and responsively. Filibusters and holds are not just arcane rules; they undermine the legislative process and make government less effective.

- Finally, beware of nonprofit political groups bearing independent presidential candidates and balanced, centrist tickets. Americans hate political parties in general but the parties are essential vehicles to represent their values and views and to give direction and purpose to government. A democracy cannot float above politics; politics—and parties—are critical components of our democratic DNA. Political groups promoting the siren song of transcending politics instead of working to change the dysfunctional behavior of those in politics and government suffer from their own democratic deficit and are more likely to play spoiler or produce an ungovernable administration than to remedy dysfunctional politics.

Conclusion

A Westminster-style parliamentary system provides a much cleaner form of democratic accountability than the American system. A party or coalition of parties forms a government after an election and is in a position in parliament to put most of its program in place. The minority party will be aggressively adversarial, but it is unable to indefinitely delay or defeat the government's program. When the next election arrives (not quickly, as in the U.S., before that program has made itself felt, but in four or five years), there is no confusion in the public over which party is to be held accountable. If the government is thrown out of office, the minority party can govern on its own terms, within an institutional setting and political culture that accepts the legitimacy of the new government and the policy changes that will follow.

As we write this book, the United States is approaching a pivotal election without that clarity. Voters, as disgruntled with the performance of Congress and the policy dynamic in Washington as at any point in our lifetimes, are expecting and hoping that their collective voice will be heard and accountability achieved.

But how? We fear that expectations in 2012 will not be reached, and that the range of potential outcomes do not easily allow for one that will either affirm the existing order or accomplish sweeping change, at least in a way that will recreate a functional and legitimate political process. If President Obama gets reelected but faces either a continuing divided Congress or a Congress with Republicans in charge of both houses, there is little reason to expect a new modus vivendi in which the president and GOP leaders are able to find reasonable compromises in areas like budget policy, health reform and financial regulation.

If President Obama is reelected and sees his party recapture the House and hold its majority in the Senate, there is some reason to believe that the dynamic will change. Republicans will have suffered an unexpected and devastating defeat, and some Republican Senators may decide the time has come to put the all-out opposition strategy aside and re-engage in the lawmaking process. Less ideological and more pragmatic leaders may begin to emerge in the GOP. Obama might be able to use the expiring Bush tax cuts as a basis to entice a number of Senate Republicans into a revenue-producing tax reform process and efforts to strengthen cost-savings initiatives in Medicare and Medicaid.

It is also possible that Senate Republicans will return to the use of filibusters and holds to slow down the process, obstruct the president's appointments, and make every policy victory a protracted and ugly battle to delegitimize the outcome, hoping for another sweeping victory in the 2014 midterms akin to what they achieved in 2010.

If President Obama loses his reelection bid and Republicans hold the House and win the Senate, with narrow majorities much like the ones George W. Bush had in his first year as president in 2001, the new Republican government will certainly use the tools Bush did, starting with budget reconciliation, to promote a sweeping agenda that will start with dismantling health reform, gutting financial regulation, cutting taxes even more, and making deep cuts in domestic spending. There are limits to what can be done with budget reconciliation (although the tool was used to achieve the huge tax cuts in 2001 and 2003 that contributed mightily to our long-term debt crisis). Senate Democrats will be tempted in many or most cases to use filibusters and holds to limit the damage, and there will be a strong temptation on Mitch McConnell's part to act unilaterally to erase the filibuster to take advantage of this rare chance to achieve revolutionary change.

Under those circumstances, we could potentially see major policy shifts, indeed revolutionary ones, akin to those that are frequent in parliamentary systems. But even more than in the first two years of the Obama administration, the changes—deeper tax cuts; steep reductions in Medicaid through block grants to the states; partial privatization of Social Security; massive deregulation in finance and environmental policy—would come to a country that is deeply divided politically, and more than half of whose citizens would likely strongly oppose these moves and be jolted by their implementation. The schisms created could be greater than any we have seen in more than a century.

We do not mean to suggest that it would mean the end of America as we know it; the country, with its deep patriotism, enormous reservoir of talent and belief in freedom, and inherent flexibility to respond and adapt to crisis, would survive and ultimately come back as it has in the past. But because we face enormous challenges—emerging from the deepest downturn since the Great Depression; solving our looming deficit and debt problems; finding ways to create jobs while competing in an increasingly challenging global economy; and ensuring that the burdens from our aging population do not overwhelm our capacity to respond—the prospect that we might have to adapt to these challenges, with an even more dysfunctional or discredited political system means that all Americans who care about solving or tackling these problems should take our proscriptions and prescriptions seriously.

To be sure there are some signs of green shoots sprouting throughout the country. One is the model set by our metropolitan areas—fifty-one of which have populations greater than one million—that are finding public-private partnerships and cross-party alliances to solve their problems in transportation, social welfare, education, and infrastructure. Another is that, even in this awful political environment, some of the best and brightest and most admirable in our society are still stepping forward to do public service and to run for political office. A third is the number of former lawmakers, especially Republicans, who are mad as hell and determined to change things in the system and in their own party. They are joined by a handful of influential conservative public intellectuals who are questioning the take-no-prisoners, no compromise position that has taken over the GOP. A fourth is in the new social movements, including both the Tea Party and Occupy Wall Street. If their goals are sometimes amorphous, their hangers-on sometimes unsettling, and their means sometimes questionable, they still reflect a broader, bottom public desire to get America back on track.

We end where we began: it *is* even worse than it looks. But we are confident that if the worst has not yet hit, better times, and a return to a better political system, do indeed lie ahead.

Acknowledgments

This book, like its 2006 predecessor, *The Broken Branch*, had its origin in an invitation from Tim Bartlett, then editor at Oxford University Press and now with Basic Books, to write a book addressing problematic features of American democracy that would be accessible to a broad public audience. In 2006 the focus was on the institutional shortcomings of Congress. This book deals more ambitiously with the country's overall dysfunctional politics. Tim's proposal to us in August 2011—that we write a short book very quickly that captured the dynamic of our governing problems and outlined a strategy for overcoming them— was audacious but, in the end, very attractive. His guidance, editing, and support were essential components of the book's timely completion.

Ours is not a report on new, original research but an extended essay that synthesizes the work of countless others and reflects years of our own Washington-watching and discussions with dear colleagues. The former is reflected in the large number of endnotes. The latter includes Sarah Binder, E.J. Dionne Jr, Bill Galston, Pietro Nivola, and Darrell West at Brookings, and Karlyn Bowman at AEI. Others who generously read all or parts of the manuscript were Al Franken, John Kingdon, Ryan Lizza, Sheilah Mann, David Price, and Michael Robinson.

We would like to offer special thanks to Raffaela Wakeman, who worked closely with us on the book and the inaugural World Forum on Governance during a very busy fall—even as she juggled the heavy workload from a first year at Georgetown Law School. Others who provided valuable assistance were Eric Glickman, Chris Lin, and Ross Tilchin at Brookings and Jennifer Marsico and Andrew Rugg at AEI.

Thanks also to the rest of our talented team at Basic Books, including Sarah Rosenthal and Caitlin Graf, and to Mark Corsey and Jane Gebhart at Eclipse Publishing Services.

Finally, a note of heartfelt thanks to the many present and former members of Congress, Republicans and Democrats, who have been constructive mentors and occasional targets of our broadsides. We especially want to thank the Republicans, moderate and conservative, who were role models of constructive engagement and patriotic problem-solving, including the late Barber Conable and Bill Steiger, along with people like Howard Baker, Bob Bennett, Sherry Boehlert, Jack Buechner, Mike Castle, Bob Dole, Mickey Edwards, Bill Frenzel, Chuck Hagel, Nancy Kassebaum, Ray LaHood, Connie Morella, John Porter, Al Simpson, Vin Weber, and too many others to recount. You are all missed in the political arena—and if you were still there and as effective as you were, this book would be unnecessary.

While we stand on the shoulders of many, we alone are responsible for whatever errors and misjudgments remain.

Notes

Introduction

1 155 Cong. Rec. S5342 (daily ed. May 12, 2009) (statement of Sen. McConnell on the Trustees Annual Report).

2 Fred Hiatt, "McConnell's cynical flip," *Washington Post*, February 1, 2010.

3 Jeff Zeleny and Megan Thee-Brenan, "New Poll Finds a Deep Distrust of Government," *New York Times*, October 26, 2011.

4 Austin Ranney, "Toward a More Responsible Two-Party System: A Commentary," *American Political Science Review* 45 (September 1951): 488–499; "Toward a More Responsible Two-Party System: A Report of the Committee on Political Parties," *American Political Science Review* 44, no. 3 (1950): part 2, supplement.

Chapter 1

1 *Economist*, "Downgrading our politics," August 6, 2011, http://www.economist.com/blogs/freeexchange/2011/08/sps-credit-rating-cut.

2 Remarks of Federal Reserve Chairman Ben S. Bernanke at the Federal Reserve Bank of Kansas City Economic Symposium, Jackson Hole, Wyoming, "The Near- and Longer-Term Prospects for the U.S. Economy," August 26, 2011, http://www.federalreserve.gov/newsevents/speech/bernanke20110826a.htm.

3 Michael Cooper and Megan Thee-Brenan, "Disapproval Rate for Congress at Record 82% After Debt Talks," *New York Times*, August 4, 2011, http://www.nytimes.com/2011/08/05/us/politics/05poll.html.

4 D. Andrew Austin and Mindy R. Levit, "The Debt Limit: History and Recent Increases," Congressional Research Service, September 9, 2011, http://www.senate.gov/CRSReports/crs-publish.cfm?pid=%270E%2C*P\%3F%3D%23%20%20%20%0A.

5 Greg Brown, "Druckenmiller Fears a Beltway Deal on Debt, Not US Default," *Money News*, May 17, 2011, http://www.moneynews.com/StreetTalk/us-economy-Druckenmiller-Beltway/2011/05/17/id/396689.

6 We draw on excellent reporting by a *Washington Post* team: Brady Dennis, Alec MacGillis, and Lori Montgomery, "Origins of the debt showdown," *Washington Post*, August 6, 2011, http://www

.washingtonpost.com/business/economy/origins-of-the-debt
-showdown/2011/08/03/gIQA9uqIzI_story.html.

7   Steve Benen, "Boehner Wants Congress to Tackle Debt Limit As
'Adults,'" *Washington Monthly*, November 19, 2010, http://www
.washingtonmonthly.com/archives/individual/2010_11/026714.php.

8   Dennis, MacGillis, and Montgomery, "Origins."

9   David M. Herszenhorn and Helene Cooper, "Concessions and Tension,
Then a Deal," *New York Times*, April 9, 2011, http://www.nytimes
.com/2011/04/10/us/politics/10reconstruct.html?pagewanted=all.

10 Patricia Murphy, "Why Eric Cantor Bailed," *Daily Beast*, June 23,
2011, http://www.thedailybeast.com/articles/2011/06/23/eric-cantor
-departure-from-biden-budget-sessions-prompted-by-obama-boehner
-talks.html.

11 David Rogers, "Debt Talks Turn to Tax Reform," *Politico*, July 7,
2011, http://www.politico.com/news/stories/0711/58535.html.

12 Lisa Mascaro and Kathleen Hennessey, "Boehner-Cantor rivalry affect-
ing debt talks," *Los Angeles Times*, July 11, 2011, http://articles
.latimes.com/2011/jul/11/nation/la-na-cantor-boehner-20110712.

13 Felicia Sonmez, "McConnell Warns Default Could 'Destroy' GOP
Brand," *Washington Post*, July 13, 2011, http://www.washingtonpost
.com/blogs/2chambers/post/mcconnell-warns-default-could-destroy
-gop-brand/2011/07/13/gIQAPZTwCI_blog.html.

14 Mike Allen, "Politico Playbook," July 20, 2011, *Politico*,
http://www.politico .com/playbook/0711/playbook1485.html.

15 David Rogers, "Debt deal momentum builds as House resists,"
Politico, July 19, 2011, http://www.politico.com/news/stories/0711/
59421.html.

16 Peter Nicholas and Lisa Mascaro, "How the Obama-Boehner debt
talks collapsed," *Los Angeles Times*, July 22, 2011, http://articles
.latimes.com/2011/jul/22/nation/la-na-obama-boehner-20110723.

17 Jay Newton-Small, "The Inside Story of Obama and Boehner's Second
Failed Grant Bargain," *Time* Swampland, July 23, 2011, http://
swampland.time.com/2011/07/23/the-inside-story-of-obama-and
-boehners-second-failed-grand-bargain/.

18 Ibid.

19 Ibid.

20 Address by President Barack Obama to the Nation, July 25, 2011,
http://www.whitehouse.gov/the-press-office/2011/07/25/address
-president-nation.

21 *Washington Post, PostPolitics*, "In debt deal, the triumph of the old
Washington," August 8, 2011, http://www.washingtonpost.com
/politics/in-debt-deal-the-triumph-of-the-old-washington/2011/08
/02/gIQARSFfqI_story_1.html. Italics added.

22 Alex Seitz-Wald, "Mitch McConnell Vows to Hold Debt Ceiling
Hostage in the Future: 'We'll Be Doing It All Over,'" *Think Progress*,
August 1, 2011, http://thinkprogress.org/politics/2011/08/01/285025
/mcconnell-vows-to-hold-debt-ceiling-hostage-again/. Italics added.

23 *Washington Post, PostPolitics,* "In debt deal, the triumph of the old
    Washington," August 8, 2011, http://www.washingtonpost.com
    /politics/in-debt-deal-the-triumph-of-the-old-washington/2011/08/02
    /gIQARSFfqI_story_1.html. Emphasis is the authors'.
24 See, for example, Pat Toomey, "The Truth About the Debt Ceiling
    and Default," *RealClearPolitics,* April 22, 2011, http://www
    .realclearpolitics.com/articles/2011/04/22/the_truth_about_the
    _debt_ceiling_and_default_109633.html; Sam Stein, "Tim Pawlenty:
    GOP Should Vote Against Raising Debt Ceiling, Then Pass Bill Pre-
    venting Default," *Huffington Post,* January 16, 2011, http://www
    .huffingtonpost.com/2011/01/16/pawlenty-debt-ceiling_n_809633
    .html; and James Freeman, "What If the U.S. Treasury Defaults," *Wall
    Street Journal,* May 14, 2011, http://online.wsj.com/article
    /SB10001424052748703864204576317612323790964.html.

Chapter 2

 1 This story is recounted in Thomas E. Mann and Norman J. Ornstein,
    The Broken Branch (New York: Oxford University Press, 2006),
    pp. 64–122.
 2 Richard F. Fenno, "If, as Ralph Nader Says, Congress Is 'The Broken
    Branch,' How Come We Love Our Congressmen So Much?" In *Con-
    gress in Change: Evolution and Reform,* ed. Norman J. Ornstein
    (New York: Praeger, 1975).
 3 Peter Osterlund, "A Capitol Chameleon: What Will Newt Gingrich
    Do Next?" *Los Angeles Times,* August 25, 1991.
 4 David Osborne, "Newt Gingrich: Shining Knight of the Post-Reagan
    Right," *New Republic,* November 1, 1984.
 5 Kim Geiger, "U.S. Chamber of Commerce launches Boxer attack ads,"
    Los Angeles Times, October 19, 2010, http://articles.latimes.com
    /2010/oct/19/news/la-pn-chamber-california-ad-20101019.
 6 Hendrik Hertzberg, "Alt-Newt," *New Yorker,* December 19, 2011,
    p. 38, http://www.newyorker.com/talk/comment/2011/12/19
    /111219taco_talk_hertzberg#ixzz1gKkpYaGl.
 7 Andy Barr, "John Shadegg, Joe Scarborough laugh at J.D. Hayworth,"
    Politico, February 25, 2010, http://www.politico.com/news/stories/
    0210/33547.html#ixzz0gfpYPOdZ.
 8 Sean Theriault and David Rohde, "The Gingrich Senators and Party
    Polarization in the Senate," *Journal of Politics,* August 2011, DOI:
    10.1017/S0022381611000752.
 9 Joe Nocera, "The Ugliness Started with Bork," *New York Times,*
    October 22, 2011, http://www.nytimes.com/2011/10/22/opinion
    /nocera-the-ugliness-all-started-with-bork.html.
10 Keith Poole and Howard Rosenthal, "Party Polarization: 1879–2010,"
    voteview blog, March 17, 2011, http://voteview.spia.uga.edu/blog
    /?p=1292.
11 Geoffrey C. Layman, Thomas M. Carsey, and Juliana Menasce
    Horowitz, "Party Polarization in American Politics: Characteristics,

Causes, and Consequences," *Annual Review of Political Science* 9 (June 2006): 83–110.

12 Ronald Brownstein, "The Four Quadrants of Congress," *National Journal*, January 30, 2011.

13 Sinclair summarizes much of the evidence. See Barbara Sinclair, *Party Wars* (Norman: University of Oklahoma Press, 2006), pp. 22–28.

14 Morris P. Fiorina and Samuel J. Abrams, *Disconnect* (Norman: University of Oklahoma Press, 2009).

15 Most recently, Alan Abramowitz, *The Disappearing Center* (New Haven, CT: Yale University Press, 2010).

16 Nolan McCarty, Keith T. Poole, and Howard Rosenthal, "Does Gerrymandering Cause Polarization?" *American Journal of Political Science* 53, no. 3, pp. 666–680 (July 2009). Thomas E. Mann, "Polarizing the House of Representatives: How Much Does Gerrymandering Matter?" in *Red and Blue Nation? Volume I*, eds. Pietro S. Nivola and David W. Brady (Washington, DC: Brookings Institution Press, 2006).

17 The next several pages are drawn in part from Mann, "Polarizing the House of Representatives."

18 Nelson W. Polsby, *How Congress Evolves: Social Bases of Institutional Change* (New York: Oxford University Press, 2003).

19 Gary Jacobson, "Explaining the Ideological Polarization of the Congressional Parties Since the 1970s," April 2004, SSRN, http://papers.ssrn.com/sol3/papers.cfm?abstract_id=1157024.

20 Bill Bishop, *The Big Sort* (New York: Houghton Mifflin Harcourt, 2008).

21 Sinclair, *Party Wars*.

22 David Rohde, *Parties and Leaders in the Postreform House* (Chicago: University of Chicago Press, 1991); Aldrich & Rohde, "Measuring Conditional Party Government," Midwest Political Science Association, April 23–25, 1998, http://www.duke.edu/~dcross/Aldrich3.pdf.

23 Sarah Binder and Thomas E. Mann, "Constraints on Leadership in Washington," *Issues in Governance Studies* 41 (July 2011), Brookings Institution.

24 Frances E. Lee, *Beyond Ideology: Politics, Principles and Partisanship in the U.S. Senate* (Chicago: University of Chicago Press, 2009).

25 Nolan McCarty, Keith T. Poole, and Howard Rosenthal, *Polarized Politics: The Dance of Ideology and Unequal Riches* (Cambridge, MA: MIT Press, 2008). Much of this is summarized in Sinclair, *Party Wars*, chapter 2; Jacob S. Hacker and Paul Pierson, *Off Center: The Republican Revolution and the Erosion of American Democracy* (New Haven, CT: Yale University Press, 2006); Geoffrey Kabaservice, *Rule and Ruin: The Downfall of Moderation and the Destruction of the Republican Party, From Eisenhower to the Tea Party* (New York: Oxford University Press, 2012).

26 Kabaservice, *Rule and Ruin*, p. xvi.

27 See, for example, John H. Makin and Norman J. Ornstein, *Debt and Taxes* (New York: Times Books, 1994).

28 Cameron Joseph, "Former GOP Sen. Hagel bashes Republicans," *The Hill Ballot Box*, September 1, 2011, http://thehill.com/blogs /ballot-box/senate-races/179243-republican-former-senator-hagel -bashes-gop.

29 Mike Lofgren, "Goodbye to All That: Reflections of a GOP Operative Who Left the Cult," *Truthout*, http://www.truth-out.org/goodbye-all -reflections-gop-operative-who-left-cult/1314907779.

30 Frank Newport, "Very Conservative Americans: Leaders Should Stick to Beliefs," Gallup Poll, January 12, 2011, http://www.gallup.com/poll /145541/conservative-americans-leaders-stick-beliefs.aspx.

31 Theda Skocpol and Lawrence Jacobs, eds., *Reaching for a New Deal: Ambitious Governance, Economic Meltdown, and Polarized Politics in Obama's First Two Years* (New York: Russell Sage Foundation, 2011).

32 Gallup Poll, op. cit.

33 Galston and Mann, "The GOP's grass-roots obstructionists" *Washington Post*, May 16, 2010, http://www.washingtonpost.com/wp-dyn /content/article/2010/05/14/AR2010051404234.html.

34 Poole and Rosenthal, "Party Polarization."

35 Adam Bonica, "Introducing the 112th Congress," *Ideological Cartography*, November 5, 2010, http://ideologicalcartography.com/2010 /11/05/introducing-the-112th-congress/.

36 Much of the analysis in this section comes from Norman Ornstein with John C. Fortier and Jennifer Marsico, "Creating a Public Square in a Challenging Media Age: A White Paper on the Knight Commission Report on Informing Communities: Sustaining Democracy in the Digital Age" (Washington, DC: AEI, 2011), http://www.knightcomm .org/wp-content/uploads/2011/06/CreatingaPublicSquare.pdf.

37 Adam Thierer, "Submission to Participants in Knight Foundation/AEI Workshop on the Information Needs of Communities in a Digital Age," paper presented at AEI discussion and working lunch, April 12, 2010, p. 4.

38 Ibid., p. 4.

39 See, for example, Martin Kaplan and Matthew Hale, "Local TV News in the Los Angeles Media Market: Are Stations Serving the Public Interest?" (Los Angeles: The Norman Lear Center, March 11, 2010).

40 David Carr and Tim Arango, "A Fox Chief at the Pinnacle of Media and Politics," *New York Times*, January 9, 2010, http://www.nytimes .com/2010/01/10/business/media/10ailes.html?pagewanted=1&hp.

41 Pew Research Center, "Partisanship and Cable News Audiences," October 30, 2009, http://pewresearch.org/pubs/1395/partisanship -fox-news-and-other-cable-news-audiences.

42 VisionCritical, "The Politics of Cable News: Do Americans believe Fox News qualifies as News?" October 22, 2009, http://www .visioncritical.com/2009/10/the-politics-of-cable-news-do-americans -believe-fox-news-qualifies-as-news/.

43 The Winthrop Poll, http://www.winthrop.edu/winthroppoll/default .aspx?id=9804.

44 This analysis comes in significant part from Norman Ornstein, "The Rumored Perks of Congressional Service," *Roll Call*, May 11, 2011, http://www.rollcall.com/issues/56_120/ornstein_rumored_perks _congressional_service-205495-1.html.

45 Patrick J. Purcell, "Retirement Benefits for Members of Congress," *Congressional Research Service*, February 9, 2007, http://www .senate.gov/reference/resources/pdf/RL30631.pdf.

46 FactCheck.org, "Congress Not Exempt from Student Loans," January 6, 2011, http://www.factcheck.org/2011/01/congress-not-exempt -from-student-loans/.

47 Barbara English, "Health Benefits for Members of Congress," Congressional Research Service, September 25, 2007, http://mcmorris.house .gov/uploads/August2009HealthCareBenefitsforMembersofCongress .PDF.

48 Paul Farhi, "The email rumor mill is run by conservatives," *Washington Post*, November 17, 2011.

49 Robert G. Kaiser, *So Much Damn Money: The Triumph of Lobbying and the Corrosian of American Government* (New York: Knopf, 2009).

50 *60 Minutes* transcript, http://thinkprogress.org/special/2011/11/07 /362392/abramoff-owned-congress/. Italics added.

51 Anthony Corrado, "Money and Politics: A History of Federal Campaign Finance Law," in *The New Campaign Finance Sourcebook*, eds. Anthony Corrado, Daniel R. Ortiz, Thomas E. Mann, and Trevor Potter (Washington, DC: Brookings Institution Press, 2005), p. 7.

52 This section adapted from Norman Ornstein, "Court Way Oversteps Its Authority with Citizens United Case," *Roll Call*, January 27, 2010, http://www.rollcall.com/issues/55_82/-42639-1.html.

53 Associated Press, "Chief Justice Says His Goal Is More Consensus On Court," May 22, 2006, http://www.nytimes.com/2006/05/22 /washington/22justice.html.

54 Richard L. Hasen, "How Justice Kennedy paved the way for "Super-PACS" and the return of soft money," *Slate*, October 25, 2011, http://www.slate.com/articles/news_and_politics/jurisprudence/2011 /10/citizens_united_how_justice_kennedy_has_paved_the_way_for _the_re.html.

55 Brennan Center for Justice, New York University School of Law, "Outside Groups Dominate Spending in Judicial Elections, New Report Shows," press release, October 26, 2011, http://www.brennancenter .org/content/resource/outside_groups_dominate_spending_in _judicial_elections_new_report_shows.

56 Kenneth P. Vogel, "Rove-linked group uses secret donors to fund attacks," *Politico*, July 21, 2010, http://www.politico.com/news /stories/0710/39998.html.

57 Ibid.

58 *SpeechNow v. Federal Election Commission*, 599 F.3d 686 (C.A.D.C. 2010).

59 Democracy21, "Leading Presidential-Candidate Super PACs and The Serious Questions that Exist About Their Legality," January 4, 2011, http://www.democracy21.org/vertical/Sites/%7B3D66FAFE-2697 -446F-BB39-85FBBBA57812%7D/uploads/Democracy_21_Super _PAC_Report__1_4_2012.pdf.

60 Maggie Haberman, "Mystery Mitt Romney donor comes forward," *Politico*, August 8, 2011, http://www.politico.com/news/stories/0811 /60776.html.

61 Ibid.

62 Laylan Copelin, "Perry has long history with super PAC friend," *Austin American-Statesman*, September 15, 2011, http://www .statesman.com/news/texas-politics/perry-has-long-history-with-super -pac-friend-1861325.html.

63 This section draws on Norman Ornstein, "Citizens United: Corrupting Campaign Clarity," *Roll Call*, June 15, 2011, http://www.rollcall .com/issues/56_139/citizens_united_corrupting_campaign_clarity -206476-1.html.

64 Jane Mayer, "State for Sale," *New Yorker*, October 10, 2011, http:// www.newyorker.com/reporting/2011/10/10/111010fa_fact_mayer.

65 Paul Herrnson, "The Roles of Party Organizations, Party-Connected Committees, and Party Allies in Elections," *Journal of Politics* 71 (October 2009): 1207–1224.

66 In a column focusing on the conflict between the Montana Supreme Court's recent opinion upholding a state ban on corporate contributions, Dahlia Lithwick wonders whether the decision will go to the U.S. Supreme Court. See Dahlia Lithwick, "In Montana, Corporations Aren't People," *Slate*, January 4, 2012, http://www.slate.com/articles /news_and_politics/jurisprudence/2012/01/montana_supreme_court _citizens_united_can_montana_get_away_with_defying_the_supreme _court_.html.

Chapter 3

1 Edward S. Corwin, *The President: Office and Powers* (New York: New York University Press, 1957), p. 171.

2 The FAA story is described in detail in a *Washington Post* story and an earlier *Post* blog entry: Ashley Halsey III, "FAA shutdown imperils billions in projects," *Washington Post*, July 30, 2011, http://www .washingtonpost.com/local/faa-shutdown-imperils-billions-in -projects/2011/07/29/gIQAvmC5jI_story.html; Dylan Matthews, "Everything you need to know about the FAA shutdown in one post," *Washington Post Online, Ezra Klein's Wonkblog*, August 3, 2011, http://www.washingtonpost.com/blogs/ezra-klein/post/everything -you-need-to-know-about-the-faa-shutdown-in-one-post/2011/07/11 /gIQAfatTsI_blog.html.

3 See, for example, Norman Ornstein, "Our Broken Senate," *The American*, March/April 2008, http://www.american.com/archive/2008 /march-april-magazine-contents/our-broken-senate; *Examining the*

Filibuster: The Filibuster Today and its Consequences, before the Senate Committee on Rules and Administration, 111th Cong. (168) (statement of Norman Ornstein, Resident Scholar, American Enterprise Institute).

4 Sarah Binder and Steven Smith, *Politics or Principle? Filibustering in the United States Senate* (Washington, DC: Brookings Institution Press, 1997), pp. 29–39.

5 Ibid, p. 38.

6 United States Senate, Senate Action on Cloture Motions, http://www .senate.gov/pagelayout/reference/cloture_motions/clotureCounts.htm.

7 Sarah Binder, "Through the Looking Glass, Darkly: What has Become of the Senate?" *Forum 9*, no. 4 (2011), http://www.bepress.com/forum /vol9/iss4/art2/.

8 This arms race between the parties is described well by Steven Smith in "The Senate Syndrome," *The Brookings Institution Issues in Governance Studies*, no. 35, http://www.brookings.edu/papers/2010/06 _cloture_smith.aspx.

9 Francis E. Lee, "Making Laws and Making Points: Senate Governance in an Era of Uncertain Majorities," *Forum 9*, no. 4, pp. 1–17. "Parties as Problem Solvers," in *Promoting the General Welfare*, Alan S. Gerber and Eric M. Patashnik, eds. (Washington, DC: Brookings Institution Press, 2006), pp. 237–255.

10 U.S. Senate, 2009, *Worker, Homeownership, and Business Assistance Act*, H.R. 3548. 111th Cong., 1st sess. Roll Call Vote No. 334, November 4, 2009, S.11099-11103; U.S. Senate, 2009, *Worker, Homeownership, and Business Assistance Act*, H.R. 3548. 111th Cong., 1st sess. Roll Call Vote No. 329, October 27, 2009, S.10769-10772; U.S. Senate, 2009, *Worker, Homeownership, and Business Assistance Act*, H.R. 3548. 111th Cong., 1st sess. Roll Call Vote No. 333, November 4, 2009, S.11080.

11 U.S. Senate, 2009, *Credit Cardholders' Bill of Rights Act*, H.R. 627. 111th Cong., 1st sess. Roll Call Vote No. 193, May 19, 2009, S.5570; U.S. Senate, 2009, *Credit Cardholders' Bill of Rights Act*, H.R. 627. 111th Cong., 1st sess. Roll Call Vote No. 194, May 19, 2009, S.5573-5581.

12 U.S. Senate, 2009, *Fraud Enforcement Recovery Act*, S.386. 111th Cong., 1st sess. Roll Call Vote No. 170, April 27, 2009, S.4740; U.S. Senate, 2009, *Fraud Enforcement Recovery Act*, S.386. 111th Cong., 1st sess. Roll Call Vote No. 171, April 27, 2009, S.4777-4781.

13 American Constitution Society ACS Blog, "After Five Months, Senators Unanimously Confirm Fourth Circuit Nominee," March 2, 2010, http://www.acslaw.org/acsblog/all/justice-barbara-keenan.

14 The following section has been taken in major part from testimony given to the Senate Rules Committee by Thomas E. Mann on June 23, 2010.

15 *Examining the Filibuster: Silent Filibusters, Holds, and the Senate Confirmation Process, before the Senate Committee on Rules and Admin-*

istration, 111th Cong. (336) (statement of G. Calvin Mackenzie, Goldfarb Family Distinguished Professor of Government, Department of Government, Colby College).

16 E.J. Dionne and William A. Galston, "A Half-Empty Government Can't Govern: Why Everyone Wants to Fix the Appointments Process, Why it Never Happens, and How We Can Get It Done," Brookings Institution, December 14, 2010, http://www.brookings.edu/papers /2010/1214_appointments_galston_dionne.aspx.

17 Jonathan Cohn, "The New Nullification: GOP v. Obama Nominees," *New Republic*, July 19, 2011, http://www.tnr.com/blog/jonathan -cohn/92167/cordray-warren-cfpb-obama-republicans-nomination.

18 Mann, Testimony, June 23, 2010.

19 Caroline May, "Obama caves, surrenders top Medicare administrator," *Daily Caller*, November 23, 2011, http://dailycaller.com/2011/11/23 /obama-caves-surrenders-top-medicare-administrator/#ixzz1ekess900.

20 Alfred Stepan and Juan J. Linz, "Comparative Perspectives on Inequality and the Quality of Democracy in the United States," *Perspectives on Politics* 9, no. 4 (December 2011), DOI: 10.1017 /S1537592711003756.

21 Daniel Patrick Moynihan articulated this concept in "Defining Deviancy Down," *American Scholar* 62, no. 1 (Winter 1993): 17–30.

Chapter 4

1 David R. Mayhew, *Divided We Govern: Party Control, Lawmaking, and Investigations, 1946–2002* (New Haven, CT: Yale University Press, 2005).

2 Sarah Binder, *Stalemate: Causes and Consequences of Legislative Gridlock* (Washington, DC: Brookings Institution Press, 2003).

3 David R. Mayhew, *Partisan Balance: Why Political Parties Don't Kill the U.S. Constitutional System* (Princeton, NJ: Princeton University Press, 2011), p. 14.

4 Ibid, p. 190.

5 Abraham Lincoln's election in 1860 coincided with the emergence of a new Republican party to replace the failed Whigs.

6 Thomas L. Friedman, "Make Way for the Radical Center," *New York Times*, July 23, 2011, http://www.nytimes.com/2011/07/24/opinion /sunday/24friedman.html; Thomas L. Friedman, "A Tea Party Without Nuts," *New York Times*, March 23, 2010, http://www.nytimes.com /2010/03/24/opinion/24friedman.html; Thomas L. Friedman and Michael Mandelbaum, *That Used to Be Us: How America Fell Behind in the World It Invented and How We Can Come Back* (New York: Farrar, Straus and Giroux, 2011).

7 Ezra Klein, "Do we need a third-party presidential candidacy? A de-bate with Matt Miller," *Washington Post*, October 18, 2011, http:// www.washingtonpost.com/blogs/ezra-klein/post/do-we-need-a-third -party-presidential-candidacy-a-debate-with-matt-miller/2011/08/25 /gIQApOV8uL_blog.html; Matt Miller, "The third-party stump

speech we need," *Washington Post*, September 25, 2011, http://www
.washingtonpost.com/opinions/the-third-party-stump-speech-we
-need/2011/09/22/gIQAjzx8wK_print.html; Matt Miller, "Why we
need a third party of (radical) centrists," *Washington Post*, November
11, 2010, http://www.washingtonpost.com/wp-dyn/content/article
/2010/11/10/AR2010111003489.html.

8 See http://www.americanselect.org/; Nathan L. Gonzales, "Party
Crashers All the Rage, Aren't All the Same," *Roll Call*, August 17,
2011, http://www.rollcall.com/news/party_crashers_all_the_rage
_arent_all_the_same-208221-1.html.

9 Bruce E. Keith, et al., *The Myth of the Independent Voter* (Berkeley:
University of California Press, 1992).

10 Larry M. Bartels, "The Irrational Electorate," *Wilson Quarterly* 32,
no.4 (Autumn 2008): 44–50; Thomas M. Carsey, Geoffrey C.
Layman, "Changing Sides or Changing Minds? Party Identification
and Policy Preferences in the American Electorate," *American Journal
of Political Science* 50, no. 2 (April 2006): 464–477.

11 Richard Hasen, "A democracy deficit at Americans Elect?" *Politico*,
November 9, 2011, http://www.politico.com/news/stories/1111/67965
.html.

12 Matt Miller, "Why we need a third party," *Washington Post*, September 25, 2011, http://www.washingtonpost.com/opinions/why-we
-need-a-third-party/2011/09/25/gIQALQLGxK_story.html.

13 Donald Marron, "Oops! Senate Republicans' big budget mistake,"
Christian Science Monitor, July 8, 2011, http://www.csmonitor.com
/Business/Donald-Marron/2011/0708/Oops!-Senate-Republicans-big
-budget-mistake.

14 Jonathan Chait, "The Balanced Budget Scam," *New Republic*,
August 31, 2011, http://www.tnr.com/blog/jonathan-chait/94371
/the-balanced-budget-scam; Michael Linden, "Not So Fast, Newt: The
Real Heroes of the 1998 Budget Surplus: Clinton and His Economy,"
Center for American Progress, March 7, 2011, http://www.american
progress.org/issues/2011/03/newts_surplus.html.

15 CNN Money, "Greenspan eyes tax cuts," January 25, 2011,
http://money.cnn.com/2001/01/25/economy/greenspan/.

16 Bruce Bartlett, "Are the Bush Tax Cuts the Root of Our Fiscal Problem?" *New York Times Economix*, July 26, 2011 http://economix
.blogs.nytimes.com/2011/07/26/are-the-bush-tax-cuts-the-root-of
-our-fiscal-problem/.

17 Ibid.

18 See Teresa Tritch, "How the Deficit Got This Big," *New York Times*,
July 23, 2011, http://www.nytimes.com/2011/07/24/opinion/sunday
/24sun4.html.

19 Christina D. Romer, "Do Tax Cuts Starve the Beast? The Effect of Tax
Changes on Government Spending," National Bureau of Economic
Research, Working Paper No. 13548, October 2007, http://www.nber
.org/papers/w13548; Peter R. Orzag and William G. Gale, "Bush

Administration Tax Policy: Starving the Beast?" Brookings Institution, Tax Notes, November 15, 2004, http://www.brookings.edu/articles /2004/1115useconomics_gale.aspx.

20 Caroline May, "Term Limits for Congress?" *Daily Caller*, April 15, 2011, http://dailycaller.com/2011/04/15/term-limits-for-congress/.

21 George F. Will, *Restoration: Congress, Term Limits and the Recovery of Deliberative Democracy* (New York: Free Press, 1993).

22 *U.S. Term Limits, Inc. v. Thornton*, 514 U.S. 779 (1995).

23 Thad Kousser, *Term Limits and the Dismantling of State Legislative Professionalism* (New York: Cambridge University Press, 2005); "Legislative Term Limits: An Overview," National Conference of State Legislatures, accessed January 3, 2011, http://www.ncsl.org/default .aspx?tabid=14849.

24 Kousser, *Term Limits and the Dismantling of State Legislative Professionalism*; John M. Carey, Richard G. Niemi, and Lynda W. Powell, *Term Limits in State Legislatures* (Ann Arbor: University of Michigan Press, 2000); Karl T. Kurtz, Bruce Cain, and Richard G. Niemi, eds., *Institutional Change in American Politics: The Case of Term Limits; Legislating Without Experience* (Washington, DC: National Conference of State Legislatures, 2007).

25 Eliza Newton-Carney, "The Deregulated Campaign," *CQ Weekly*, September 17, 2011.

26 Lawrence Lessig, *Republic, Lost: How Money Corrupts Congress— and a Plan to Stop It* (New York: Twelve, 2011).

Chapter 5

1 The Pew Center on the States, "Upgrading Democracy: Improving America's Elections by Modernizing States' Voter Registration Systems," November 2010, http://www.pewcenteronthestates.org /uploadedFiles/Upgrading_Democracy_report.pdf.

2 Christopher Ponoroff, "Voter Registration in a Digital Age," Brennan Center for Justice, 2010, http://brennan.3cdn.net/806ab5ea23fde7c261 _n1m6b1s4z.pdf.

3 Ibid.

4 The Pew Center on the States, "Upgrading Democracy: Improving America's Elections by Modernizing States' Voter Registration Systems," November 2010, http://www.pewcenteronthestates.org /uploadedFiles/Upgrading_Democracy_report.pdf.

5 Midwest Political Science Association, with Robert M. Stein and Greg Vonnahme, "Election Day Vote Centers and Voter Turnout," Chicago, Ill., April 22–24, 2006.

6 Dēmos, "Voters Win with Election Day Registration," Winter 2008, http://archive.demos.org/pubs/Voters%20Win.pdf.

7 Eric Russell, "Mainers vote to continue Election Day registration," *Bangor Daily News*, November 8, 2011, http://bangordailynews.com /2011/11/08/politics/early-results-indicate-election-day-voter -registration-restored/.

8 Jim Davenport, "SC voter ID law hits some black precincts harder," Associated Press, October 19, 2011, http://www.boston.com/news /nation/articles/2011/10/19/sc_voter_id_law_hits_some_black _precincts_harder/.

9 Peter Wallsten, "In states, parties clash over voting laws that would affect college students, others," *Washington Post, Post Politics*, March 8, 2011, http://www.washingtonpost.com/wp-dyn/content /article/2011/03/06/AR2011030602662.html.

10 Heather K. Gerken, "A Third Way for the Voting Rights Act: Section 5 and the Opt-In Approach," Paper 354, http://digitalcommons.law.yale .edu/fss_papers/354.

11 William A. Galston, "Telling Americans to Vote, or Else" *New York Times*, November 5, 2011, http://www.nytimes.com/2011/11/06 /opinion/sunday/telling-americans-to-vote-or-else.html?pagewanted=all.

12 Norman Ornstein, "How to Expand the Center? Look Down Under," *Roll Call*, April 28, 2010, http://www.rollcall.com/issues/55_123 /-45605-1.html.

13 "Voter Turnout for Referendums and Elections 1901–Present," *Australian Electoral Commission*, accessed January 31, 2012, http://www .aec.gov.au/Elections/australian_electoral_history/Voter_Turnout.htm.

14 Thomas E. Mann, "Polarizing the House of Representatives: How Much Does Gerrymandering Matter?" in *Red and Blue Nation? Volume I*, eds. Pietro S. Nivola and David W. Brady (Washington, DC: Brookings Institution Press, 2006); Nolan McCarty, Keith T. Poole, and Howard Rosenthal, "Does Gerrymandering Cause Polarization?" *American Journal of Political Science* 53, no. 3 (July 2009): 666–680, doi: 10.1111/j.1540-5907.2009.00393.x.

15 Thomas E. Mann, "Redistricting Reform: What is Desirable? Possible?" in *Party Lines*, eds. Thomas E. Mann and Bruce Cain (Washington, DC: Brookings Institution Press, 2005).

16 Michael McDonald and Micah Altman, "Pulling back the curtain on redistricting," *Washington Post*, July 9, 2010, http://www .washingtonpost.com/wp-dyn/content/article/2010/07/08 /AR2010070804270.html.

17 Elisabeth R. Gerber and Rebecca B. Morton, "Primary Election Systems and Representation," *Journal of Law, Economics and Organization* 14, no. 2 (1998): 304–324, http://www.jstor.org/stable/765107.

18 Erin McGhee, "Open Primaries," *At Issue*, Public Policy Institute of California, February 2010, http://www.ppic.org/content/pubs /atissue/AI_210EMAI.pdf.

19 Gerber and Morton, "Primary Election Systems."

20 McGhee, "Open Primaries."

21 Maurice Duverger, "Les Partis Politique," in Universite de Bordeaux, Conferences du Lundi, 1946.

22 Robert Richie and Steven Hill, "The Case for Proportional Representation," *Boston Review*, February–March 1998, http://bostonreview .net/BR23.1/richie.html.

23 Rein Taagepera and Matthew Soberg Shugart, *Seats and Votes: The Effects and Determinants of Electoral Systems* (New Haven, CT: Yale, 1989), pp. 26–28.

24 See also Remarks by Trevor Potter, President, Campaign Legal Center to the Professional Advocacy Association of Texas, "Super PACs: How We Got Here, Where We Need to Go," Friday, December 2, 2011, http://www.clcblog.org/index.php?option=com_content&view= article&id=444:super-pacs-how-we-got-here-where-we-need-to-go.

25 Andy Kroll, "What the FEC?" *Mother Jones*, April 18, 2011, http://motherjones.com/politics/2011/04/fec-cazayoux-citizens-united.

26 Newton Minow and Henry Geller, "Who is paying for political ads?" *Politico*, December 11, 2011, http://www.politico.com/news/stories /1211/70263.html#ixzz1gHmmSnfE.

27 Ibid.

28 "The CPA-Zicklin Index of Corporate Political Accountability and Disclosure," Center for Political Accountability and The Carol and Lawrence Zicklin Center for Business Ethics Research, October 28, 2011, http://www.politicalaccountability.net/index.php?ht= a/GetDocumentAction/i/5800.

29 "Leadership PACs," Center for Responsive Politics, http://www .opensecrets.org/pacs/industry.php?txt=Q03&cycle=2012.

30 Jack Abramoff, *Capitol Punishment: The Hard Truth About Washington Corruption from America's Most Notorious Lobbyist* (Washington, DC: WND Books, 2011), p. 305.

31 Anthony Corrado et al., "Reform in an Age of Networked Campaigns: How to Foster Citizen Participation Through Small Donors and Volunteers," Brookings Institution, American Enterprise Institute, and Campaign Finance Institute, January 14, 2010, http://www .brookings.edu/reports/2010/0114_campaign_finance_reform.aspx.

Chapter 6

1 R. Kent Weaver and Bert A. Rockman, eds., *Do Institutions Matter?* (Washington, DC: Brookings Institution Press, 1993).

2 *A resolution to amend the Standing Rules of the Senate to reform the filibuster rules to improve the daily process of the Senate*, S. Res. 12, 112th Cong., 1st Session; *A resolution to improve the debate and consideration of legislative matters and nominations in the Senate*, S. Res. 10, 112th Cong., 1st Session; *A resolution to amend the Standing Rules of the Senate to provide procedures for extended debate*, S. Res. 21, 112th Cong., 1st Session.

3 Sarah Binder et al., "What Senators Need to Know about Filibuster Reform," December 2, 2010, http://www.brookings.edu/opinions /2010/1202_filibuster_mann_binder.aspx; Martin B. Gold and Dimple Gupta, "The Constitutional Option to Change Senate Rules and Procedures: A Majoritarian Means to Over Come the Filibuster," *Harvard Journal of Law & Public Policy* 28, no. 1 (2006): 206–272, http://www.law.harvard.edu/students/orgs/jlpp/Gold_Gupta_JLPP

_article.pdf; Aaron-Andrew P. Bruhl, "Burying the 'Continuing Body' Theory of the Senate," *Iowa Law Review* 95 (2010), http://www .uiowa.edu/~ilr/issues/ILR_95-5_Bruhl.pdf; Senate Committee on Rules and Administration, Hearing on "Examining the Filibuster: Silent Filibusters, Holds and the Senate Confirmation Process," June 23, 2010, pp. 390–391; Senate Judiciary Committee, Sub-committee on the Constitution, Hearing on Judicial Nominations and Filibusters, May 6, 2003.

4 Mark Tushnet, "A Political Perspective on the Theory of the Unitary Executive," *University of Pennsylvania Journal of Constitutional Law*, 2009, 12, no. 2, 313–330; Steven G. Calabresi and Christopher S. Yoo, *The Unitary Executive* (New Haven, CT: Yale University Press, 2008).

5 Russell Wheeler, unpublished paper, October 15, 2008.

6 Charles Savage, *Takeover: The Return of the Imperial Presidency and the Subversion of American Democracy* (New York: Little, Brown and Company, 2008).

7 Sarah Rosen Wartell and John Podesta, "The Power of the President: Recommendations to Advance Progressive Change," Center for American Progress, November 16, 2010, http://www.americanprogress.org /issues/2010/11/executive_orders.html.

8 Daniel Carpenter, "Free the F.D.A.," *New York Times*, December 13, 2011, http://www.nytimes.com/2011/12/14/opinion/free-the-fda.html.

9 R. Chuck Mason, "Base Realignment and Closure (BRAC): Transfer and Disposal of Military Property," Congressional Research Service, March 31, 2009, http://www.fas.org/sgp/crs/natsec/R40476.pdf.

10 Henry Aaron, "The Independent Payment Advisory Board—Con-gress's 'Good Deed,'" *New England Journal of Medicine* 364 (2011): 2377–2379, http://www.nejm.org/doi/full/10.1056/NEJMp1105144.

Chapter 7

1 Courtney Comstock, "Steve Schwarzman on Tax Increase: It's Like When Hitler Invaded Poland," *Business Insider*, August 16, 2010, http://articles.businessinsider.com/2010-08-16/wall_street/30045366 _1_tax-hikes-taxes-on-private-equity-poland.

2 Scott Rothschild, "Speaker O'Neal apologizes for forwarding email that calls Michelle Obama 'Mrs. YoMama,'" *The Lawrence Journal-World*, January 5, 2012, http://www2.ljworld.com/news/2012/jan/05 /statehouse-live-speaker-oneal-forwards-email-calls/.

3 U.S. Senate, 2012, *National Defense Authorization Act*, S.1867. 112th Cong., 1st sess. S.7943-7987, S.8012-8054, S.8060-8062, S.8094-8138, http://hdl.loc.gov/loc.uscongress/legislation.112s1867.

4 The term *insurgent outlier* was applied to the Republican Party by Stephen Skowronek at the 2011 meeting of the American Political Science Association. We took the term from him but absolve him of any responsibility for the specific interpretations and arguments we have made with it in this volume.

5 When called to task by bloggers for advancing "false equivalence" or "artificial balance," they often retreat even more aggressively to the safe practices being criticized. See, for example, James Fallows, "False Equivalence Watch, at (sigh) the WaPo Again," *Atlantic*, November 4, 2011, http://www.theatlantic.com/politics/archive/2011/11/false -equivalence-watch-at-sigh-the-wapo-again/247906/; James Fallows, "False Equivalence Watch: Et Tu, PBS?" *Atlantic*, October 22, 2011, http://www.theatlantic.com/politics/archive/2011/10/false-equivalence -watch-et-tu-pbs/247201/.

6 Three major surveys of the scholarly literature on polarization in- cluded no discussion of its partisan asymmetry. Geoffrey C. Layman, Thomas M. Carsey, and Juliana Menasce Horowitz, "Party Polariza- tion in American Politics: Characteristics, Causes, and Consequences," *Annual Review of Political Science* 9 (June 2008): pp. 83-110; Brian F. Shaffner, "Party Polarization," In *The Oxford Handbook of the Amer- ican Congress*, eds. Erick Schickler and Frances E. Lee (New York: Oxford University Press, 2011); Paul J. Quick, "A House Dividing: Understanding Polarization," *Forum* 9 no. 2 (2011), http://www .bepress.com/forum/vol9/iss2/art12.

7 Ramesh Ponnuru, "Republicans Lose Way by Misreading Bush His- tory," Bloomberg, November 14, 2011, http://www.bloomberg.com /news/2011-11-15/republicans-lose-way-misreading-bushhistory -commentary-by-ramesh-ponnuru.html#.

8 Steven F. Hayward, "Modernizing Conservatism," *Breakthrough Jour- nal*, no. 2 (Fall 2011), http://breakthroughjournal.org/content//2011 /11/modernizing_conservatism-print.html.

9 Morris P. Fiorina, "Economic retrospective voting in American national elections: A micro-analysis," *American Journal of Political Science* 22, no. 2 (May 1978): 426–443; Gary C. Jacobson, "Referen- dum: The 2006 Midterm Congressional Elections," *Political Science Quarterly* 122, no. 1 (Spring 2007): 1–24; Alan I. Abramowitz, "An Improved Model for Predicting Presidential Election Outcomes," *Political Science and Politics* 21, no. 4 (Autumn 1988): 843–847.

10 Major Garrett, "Top GOP Priority: Make Obama a One-Term Presi- dent," *National Journal*, October 29, 2010, http://nationaljournal .com/member/magazine/top-gop-priority-make-obama-a-one-term -president-20101023.

11 Larry M. Bartels, "Ideology and Retrospection in Electoral Responses to the Great Recession," prepared for a conference on "Popular Reac- tions to the Great Recession," Nuffield College, Oxford, England, June 24–26, 2011.

12 Robert Axelrod, *The Evolution of Cooperation* (New York: Basic Books, 1985).

Index

220